CEREMONIAL ENTRIES

Joseph DeRoche

Edited by Kevin Gallagher and Martha Collins

Introduction by Martha Collins

Červená Barva Press
Somerville, Massachusetts

Červená Barva Press
P.O. Box 440357
W. Somerville, MA 02144-3222

www.cervenabarvapress.com

Bookstore: www.thelostbookshelf.com

Cover Art: Coronation of the Virgin by Fra Angelico (1434-1435)
The Yorck Project (2002)

Cover Design: William J. Kelle

ISBN: 978-1-950063-32-1

Library of Congress Control Number: 2019937330

ACKNOWLEDGMENTS

This volume would not have been possible without the work of others. First and foremost we wish to thank the late Marion Taylor—poet, friend, and former student of Joe's. When Joe passed it was Marion who located and collated all of his work and passed it on to Kevin, who serves as Joe's literary executor. Kevin also thanks Martha Collins for her introduction, fellow editing, support, and archeological digging; and Matthew Zahnzinger and Alleliah Amabelle Nuguid for their help in setting the manuscript.

Some of these poems appeared in the following journals: *Poetry Northwest, The Antioch Review, Focus/Midwest, The Iowa Review, New York Quarterly, The North American Review, Northeast, Satire Newsletter, New York Quarterly, Stone Soup, Waves, Compost, Spectrum, Frank, Imprimateur, Yankee,* and the *Heath Introduction to Poetry* (various editions). *The Inhabited Scroll* was published by Northeastern University Press, 1968.

For those who have been anticipating this volume, Kevin is sorry that it took such a long time. Most of Joe's work was not electronic and had to be typed in from paper copies and triple checked. We have tried to stay true to our understanding of the chronology of DeRoche's work. Each of the first five books represented in this volume was a full manuscript prepared by him for his MFA thesis and/or submitted to publishers—though only *The Inhabited Scroll* and *Saints* were published. There were numerous poems that kept showing up in each manuscript, with slight changes along the way. The rule of thumb we adopted was to put the poem in the book where the poem last appeared—with the exception of the poems in *The Inhabited Scroll*. This choice was made because *The Inhabited Scroll* was a published book and the versions that later appeared in *The Magic Show* were not changed. We have titled the last section of uncollected poems *The Juke Box*, because Gallagher and colleagues published the title poem in the 1990s in our magazine *Compost* and it seemed apt for this compilation of uncollected poems that DeRoche had typed and was showing to others. It also seemed apt to name this entire collection *Ceremonial Entries*, based on the title of Joe's MFA thesis, and the way he approached his life and work in general.

The two poems omitted from *Ceremonial Entry* that were included in *The Inhabited Scroll* (and are here reprinted in that section) are "Mistress Bradford before Plymouth" and "Welcomed into Foreign Rooms."

As the reader may notice, the first three poems in *Holy Orders* are taken from the MFA thesis poem "Small Pieces of a Big Mosaic." *Holy Orders* originally included four poems from *The Inhabited Scroll*, and five poems that were later included in *The Magic Show* and are here reprinted with that collection: " Poem for the Girl. . .," "Wearing My Alaskan Real Seal Parka," "Once More That Irrepressible Oh!," "Flowers," and "Aunt Laura Moves toward the Open Grave of Her Father."

The Magic Show included seven poems from earlier collections; it also included "A Little Song for Sainte Mary of Egypt," "Saint Aelred's Dance," "Therese, Therese," and "Saint Erminold," which are here published in the *Saints* sequence. Partly because it's unclear whether Joe or his editor was responsible for an altered version of the first three of these poems, this book uses the earlier versions.

Knowing that some of the uncollected poems were very likely drafts, and not wishing this collection to be substantially longer than other sections, we have limited "The Juke Box" to slightly fewer than half of the poems found in manuscript.

TABLE OF CONTENTS

Introduction by Martha Collins

CEREMONIAL ENTRY

THE INHABITED SCROLL

HOLY ORDERS

THE MAGIC SHOW

SAINTS

THE JUKE BOX

Introduction

I met Joe DeRoche in Iowa City in the 1960s. He was a poet working on an MFA in the Writers Workshop; I was a graduate student in English, beginning to think I might want to write poetry rather than write about it. Joe was from the East Coast, proud of his French-Canadian ancestry and Maine roots; a native Iowan, I'd gone to college in California and imagined that was where I'd end up. Sitting in Kenney's bar—famous for attracting students and faculty, writers and artists, some gays and lesbians—we'd talk about poetry and debate the virtues of the two coasts, often until closing time.

Joe had something to do with my ultimately deciding to write poetry, and everything to do with my moving to the East. The year after he left Iowa City to teach in Boston, he and his partner invited me for a visit that led, thanks to his hiring tips, to my getting a job in the city he loved. I thought I'd stay for a couple of years, but here I am, decades later. So writing this introduction is in some sense a repayment of a debt. It's also an act of love.

*

Joe was born and raised in Yarmouth, Maine. His father in his later years owned a restaurant that featured, if I remember correctly, lobster that he himself trapped. On his first arrival in Boston, in the 1950s, Joe followed the sounds of Handel's Water Music from the bus station to the Public Garden, where members of the Boston Symphony Orchestra were playing on swan boats. That was it, he said: Boston would be his city.

He enrolled in Northeastern University as a history major, but a professor's recitation of "Do Not Go Gentle into That Good Night" changed his life: "I was just—floored," he told Mark Mantho in 1999; "I switched my major to English and started to write poetry." After graduation, he met George Starbuck and gave him some poems. George passed them on to Anne Sexton, who wrote to Joe (as quoted, again, by Mantho): "If you keep going, learning this craft . . . you will become a great poet—I am sure of this."[1] With the encouragement of both poets, Joe went to Iowa City.

The first section of this book is, minus two poems that appear later, his Iowa MFA thesis. Many of the poems have their roots in

Maine: seacoast and beachcombers, storms and hard winters, a small coastal town deeply aware of its geography. The governing pronoun is "we," which evokes a collective presence, sometimes that of the town. There's a great deal of impressively careful observation, some of it of art, much of it of the landscape that Joe knew so well. But there are hints of what is underneath. "The Puzzle" ends like this:

> Now our improbable fingers
> plunge down from this puzzling,
> momentary hesitation to fill
> the dark space in the bushes
> where the unplanned, unsought-for,
> gathers itself to happen.

*

Joe moved back to Boston in 1965, to teach at the school where he'd discovered poetry. He taught until his retirement in 2008, and was a life-changing presence for many students, as the stunning tributes on his memorial page suggest.[2] It's no exaggeration to refer to his teaching as legendary.

Northeastern was also the source of his first and almost only published collection: *The Inhabited Scroll*, which constitutes the second section of this book, was published in 1968 as the inaugural chapbook in the "Poets at Northeastern" series. The chapbook contains only two poems from the thesis, and only one or two inhabit the Maine landscape of the earlier poems.

What replaces landscape is the beginning of an imaginative process that will govern much of Joe's poetry for decades to come. The title poem announces the change in direction as the poet imagines the other side of an ordinary green tree, a half-tree on which he carves his own figures. Most of the poems exhibit an imaginative power that, though not without tension, often feels celebratory. "Poem for the Girl Who Would Bear Flowers into the New World like Bullets" references, in its title, a hippie generation, and the process the poem describes is potentially grotesque; but the extravagance of both the gestures and the language itself render the poem a celebration of the body. "Poem" was clearly one of Joe's favorites; he included it in two subsequent collections, as well as the *Heath Introduction to Poetry*, which he began editing in 1975.

In the next few poems, the speaker dreams he is Schubert; he builds an Ark, "Not after the measurements /Of the Lord, /But after my own"; he becomes a goat, and then a giraffe. These poems of transformation are all in the first person singular, unlike so many of the earlier poems. And then there is "Simply To Say," which begins:

> You may not know this, Friend,
> But the stars came out today
> In broad daylight.
> It was wonderfully exaggerated.
> And someone kissed me
> Who promised never to do it again.

"Simply to say"—but "wonderfully exaggerated": that tension will continue to describe Joe De Roche's poetry.

*

It was after he moved back East with his partner Jim, a painter he'd met in Iowa City, that Joe's poems began to open out—first in the chapbook, then in Holy Orders, the next manuscript he put together. A poem near the end of this collection is called "In the Closet." It's set in an actual space, with sweaters and moths, but the metaphor is unmistakable.

The sections of the collection—entitled Animals, Gods, People—suggest a dialectic, but all three are permeated with desire. The dance between the sensual and the spiritual reflects Joe's Catholic heritage, and will be central to his work from now on. Many of the animals are delightfully sexual, but among those in "Medieval Tapestry: Animals Running" are "Brother Hound, Saint Hare." Conversely, the very physical gods inhabit a very physical earth: "The Wings of Angels" are "not gold. // They weigh heavy / As the feathers // Of pigeons." With a gusto that characterizes so much of this collection—ratcheted up a bit from the poems of the chapbook—Joe grants even his Maine grandparents their place among the gods in "The Return."

Reading this compilation for the first time in years, I find myself drawing little breaths of delight at first lines that are so familiar that I can recite subsequent lines without looking. "The Return" is one of those poems; "Camels, Caravans, and Myth" is another:

I've bought a fleet
Of six camels
And am leaving town
As conspicuously as I can.

And on he goes, "Like the Grand March from Aida," with white-tied men and gowned women toasting him from windows as he passes. Poems like that cheered me on as I began crafting my own.

*

Sometime before 1970, Joe began a series of moves—to New Hampshire with his partner, to Boston alone. Not long after the separation, Joe, a previously self-identified lapsed Catholic, began attending Dignity, the gay and lesbian Catholic group that was founded locally in 1972. Led by Jesuits, Dignity / Boston provided a spiritual space where both diverse sexualities and intellectual thought were embraced.

Joe collected the poems he wrote during these years in The Magic Show, which included, like the earlier collections, only a few previously-collected poems. Love and loss are in tension in The Magic Show, on scales both small and large; ultimately they're synthesized in Joe's more complete embrace of the spiritual.

The second section includes the most personal poetry he was ever to write. Beginning with poems of loss that include "The Divorced House," the section moves toward a time when, "at forty / Love began once more." These poems are plainer and more direct in style than the surrounding ones, with effectively short lines; metaphor is used memorably but sparingly. The frank treatment of love lost, found, and then "gone wild" ("The Breaking In") is both surprising and moving.

But if sexual love becomes more explicit in this collection, so does spirituality. One of the delights of reading The Magic Show is arriving at the fourth section, which includes poems for Good Friday and Easter. The "you" in "The Witches Hammer" and the Easter poem is a little shifty, but the ambiguity is part of the complex theology that Joe had begun to embrace.

The Magic Show ends with "My Father Entering Heaven"—a heaven that the speaker (unlike the "Valentine" of the previous collection) is able to envision, if only in imagination. Echoing a poem from an earlier section that looks back to his infancy, Joe concludes the collection: "Oh, my father entering heaven, / Be there to catch me."

*

In 1978, Joe was still active in Dignity, but he was also regularly visiting and going on retreat at St. Joseph's Abbey, a Trappist monastery in Spencer, Massachusetts that he had first visited in the early 1970s. A little later he was ordained in the lay Order of Saint Francis, for which he served as Formation Director from 1981 until 1993.[3] The nine "Saints" poems, which were privately published as a chapbook by a former student who also illustrated it, were written during this period in which Joe was embracing a radical version of the faith of his childhood.

The first two he wrote extend the mutual embrace of sexuality and spirituality to Sainte Mary of Egypt, "Cairo's golden whore, / An endless and revolving door," and the "Divinely gay" Saint Aelred. With their bold yet delicate balancing of sex and spirit, of humor and reverence, of intricately rhyming stanzas and quiet refrains, these remain two of my favorites of Joe's poems. But Joe took on more difficult saints as well—even "Saint Satan," who turns himself into the serpent. What Joe has accomplished in these unorthodox readings is summed up in the final poem in the series, which sanctifies "Invisible," who "Would, God knows how, have found a path / To make by stealth the Good News new."

It's worth noting that as Joe embraced traditional Christian subjects, in however unorthodox ways, he also embraced form. There are several formal poems in the MFA thesis, and a few others—including a villanelle and the terza rima "Magic Show"—in the later collections. But free or loosely accentual verse dominates until the Saints poems, all of which except "Angels" are metrical and rhyming. The delight of "Sainte Mary of Egypt" resides equally in the words themselves and in the fact that the poem is an intricately rhymed "little song."

*

Sometime in the 1990s, I lost touch with Joe, and with what he was writing; he moved to Winthrop in 1996 (he had previously lived in East Boston), and I began teaching in Ohio in 1997. By the time we reconnected, in 2006, he had dealt with a number of health problems (with more to come), and become what he called, in his letter of reconnection, a "Xtian Buddhist." So I can't date, precisely, any of the poems Kevin Gallagher has copied from Joe's papers and gathered in the last section of this book, which he has appropriately called, after the poem of that title, The Juke Box. Knowing how carefully Joe organized his earlier collections, we have made a selection from the manuscripts that attempts to provide an emotional trajectory of Joe's writing and life.

The first two poems, written later than most, serve as introduction. They're followed by "The Axer" and "We Shall Come Rejoicing," poems that I know, based on my memory and the New Hampshire setting, come from the early 1970s—as do others Kevin found that are not included here. Poems of uncertain date, probably from the mid- to late 1970s, come next, followed by formal poems, most of which I think date from the period when Joe was envisioning his Saints.[4] "The Grand Hotel" and "Reading Lips" definitely came later, the last after the 1996 move to Winthrop, where Joe could easily walk to the beach.

The final poem in this book is probably the most recent of all. In 2007, shortly after I reconnected with him, Joe sent me—along with his published volume of Saints—a sequence of six poems called "Re: Marking Orpheus," which, he said, was meant as a kind of secular companion to the Saints. "Orpheus Sings" is the last poem in that sequence.

*

But it was not his last word. In February 2011, Joe wrote me that he was "trying to write a poem about dying." "I have a part of it," he said. "I plan to call it Apophatica." That poem has not surfaced, and he mentioned no others to me after that; but what he said in the same email is an important footnote to the poems. "I would very much like to write you about the spiritual matters I am wrestling with," he said. "These writings will be personal to me and require no affirmation or denial."

Fifteen months and 20,000 words later, the series of emails was finished. In these profound and eloquent meditations, which I hope can be published someday, Joe was no more orthodox than he had ever been: he introduced me to the apophatic tradition of negative theology, which was buttressed for him by astronomy and quantum physics. But as the sensual gave way to the spiritual— partly as a result of serious illness and an accident that had nearly killed him—he was devoting himself to what a Hindu friend had called "making his soul." I'd like to end this introduction by quoting from one of these meditations:

> I still think that our motions through the universal plasma, however miniscule, have ripples through the immensity. That we belong to the Whole and that our present lives will always have been lived and cannot be erased . . . . At any rate, I have always thought that one of the fruits of mortality was that we had the pleasure of living and knowing people now that the future can only imagine and will have missed, save in the echoes that may break through into the future.

Joseph DeRoche died on April 2, 2013, just after Easter. These poems, these ceremonial entries, break through as echoes.

Martha Collins, 2018

---

1 mgmantho.files.wordpress.com/2013/08/st-joe.pdf

2 See the In Memoriam section at josephderoche.com

3 Joe told Mark Mantho that although he left the Franciscans over a "crisis of conscience," he rejected "the letter, but not the spirit, of Franciscan law."

4 Not being certain whether Joe considered all the poems in The Juke Box finished, I have taken the liberty of smoothing out the meter in a line or so of "Prayer for a Young Man" and "St. Joseph Genitor," and of making other tiny changes in "St. Joseph" and "Infant Jesus."

CEREMONIAL ENTRIES

CEREMONIAL ENTRY

Waiting in Camera

In the small room we find one chair,
a table and several bad pictures.
One Florentine woman is among them
whom we perhaps would like to meet.
Outside the room, we remember
the colorful walls, the anonymous, clear
lady. And always we return to visit.
Beyond all reason we recall this room.

Perhaps it is the cold arrangement
of flowers in the perfectly blue vase,
or the few books in the low shelves
balancing the windows and the single door.
Perhaps whoever lives here is the face
in the portrait, matches her intent,
or knows something we once knew before
we came here, something about ourselves.

This then is waiting alone, being uncertain
after the passing of music, words,
company — reconstructing what we once forgot.
We sit in the chair by the table
and watch through the window. The woods
wave behind these moving curtains;
trees dash past this small fixed spot
like proud, terrible horses going to stable.

On the table is a sheet of paper,
a pen, a crystal well brimming with ink.
We might write about visions of horses,
or a grateful note to the smiling woman
who appears kind and easy to thank.
But movement is desire and all these pictures
insinuate repeated landscapes without passion
prearranged and hung in necessary places.

The Burning of the Sonji Palace

On first glance
everyone appears
to be fleeing

and the same cart
five times repeated
is a curiosity

of chrysanthemums,
a litter of silk
bandannas. This man

masquerading so
successfully as a woman,
who sits in the cart,

whom not one Samurai
can recognize,
is, of course, the Emperor.

The four gracious ladies
seducing warriors
are his deserted concubines,

flowers of the garden.
So the palace burns
and the scroll unwinds

— a mere suggestion
of the brutal, so just
is the formality

we've grown to expect:
the royal women
attentive to love;

the skillful swordwork
of the trained soldier.

In a bellowing flame

of skirts, the Emperor
escapes North,
his eye on duty,

his costume
the burning subject
of betrayal.

The Tower

The land as you can see
was built by the ocean.
Those islands further out

— there on the horizon —
are strewn with the trunks of trees.
Storm flattens them out.

On shore we build our homes
of wood and they outlast us.
Only the tower is stone,

outsized, belonging to no one.
Unannounced the builders came,
tight-lipped men, serious.

We passed them mornings on the shore,
their blond heads lowered, always in groups.
They left and left no roof,

no steps beveled in to the door.
In the only room we sense the shape
of structure that doesn't quite come off.

The outer rounds are overgrown,
cluttered with ladders, lumber.
But, for what's here, the measurements are true:

we voted once to throw it down,
but failed, since, fitted in with care,
the stones are huge and won't undo.

Notice how the tower juts to the wind;
and note also how no stairs
lead to those two high windows

facing dead to the sea — away from land —
into those islands where no one goes

or comes from, for nothing is there.

We know it. And still recurring dreams of savages
confront us. Armies drill on those islands.
An armada, irresistible and slow, arrives.

Such yells. Such confusion of languages.
Incendiaries. No house stands.
Sea birds tower up above our lives,

spy something camouflaged, dive, circle,
cry always in that same monotony, call
until we aim and shoot and not one falls.

The Collection

After the great storm
it is easy to remain.
A man learns to sit things out.

Down in the tidal basin
wrecks wash in day after day.
In love with drift, my nephew

runs to collect it.
His sister, ingrown, spiritual,
writes stories in a perfect script.

No one enjoys her at the dinner table
or can bear the precision of her room.
We wish only to forget.

Our neighbors burn their farm
and we ignore the rain
although the huge imported roses rot

along with reason. Collections,
skeletal, organic, have a way
of growing, becoming less new,

boring, therefore, out of date.
Clutter fills the upstairs hall
and dark men with meticulous steps

avoid those scarred-up tables
piled high with shining refuse, the smell of storm
in dead things washed up bit by bit.

With Winter Before Us

Our journey has a way of stalling.
This is as far as we can come.
Outside the first hard snow is falling.

Housed in this town's dark depot
we sleep in fitful dreams of home
and when we wake we wake to snow,

to crowded benches where we turn away
from strangers as we turned from storm.
For the moment, since we're forced to stay

observe how these women have no men
hovering about them, and, struck dumb
with fear, will turn to anyone.

They know they won't survive this weather,
fictitious lovers they are stranded from.
They shall learn to be consoled by others,

perhaps by these uncertain men who wait
here with us, our enemies among them,
but honorable men, worthy of hate.

Under this selfsame roof, like it or not,
you and I must grasp at the chance to play the game
of our lives for once and act it out:

deceit and treachery and spite.
For I'm discreet and will not ask your name.
Let us now live together this one night.

Andrew Wyeth

Wyeth, how well you know my country,
how well you understand surfaces,
a wall, the color of a wall.
But artists learn that. Art is a trick,
a question of disciplines, techniques.
What I mean, Sir, is you have a secret
of another kind — where even your wall
is awkward, the light peculiar, the surfaces
lonely, desolate as in my own country.

The Beachcombers

Suspended in the tidal balance,
the calm impeccable drift
of aftermath approaches.

Fixed in this trance,
we sense the first improbable shift
of ocean to the perfect beaches.

By what our piracies uncovered,
by lost possessions
secretly reclaimed, all secrets last,

endure. Cast-offs, recovered
but transformed, confirm dead passions,
hint at some conclusive past.

Our houses are the beams of ships.
Our wives sew curtains of sheer linen
from the shirts of strangers.

We know no heroes. Whoever rips
the clothing from corrupting men
has seen them torn from what deranges,

elevates, demands commitment.
They and their household goods
come shoreward, bleached in salt water.

Surely something was meant.
Their eyes turn upward, white like stone gods',
defenseless, cold enough to shatter

should we intrude, probing for life.
The tide, the drifting objects come.
We turn to meet them coming in.

11

The sea heaves up the stuff
of lives colliding. We hack our homes
from such completed functions.

I Have Built a Bridge

On the Penobscot cliffs
facing the Atlantic East,
the sun constructs a bridge,

or is the tall twin tower,
rather, of a highway
where no one seems to walk,

no trucks convey, no cars
speed into the sunrise.
Though I desire travel

always, it's not on ships
but the passage by bridge,
the rising approaches

over cities, suburbs,
farmlands, into the air.
We climb like mountaineers

tied to our perilous ropes,
but for love's sake, to prove
something at last, like men

who stand on watch, desiring,
while that water-soaked road
shines, the passage promises,

and the surface gives way
on the first step, crumbles
in cold sheets of metal
over the swimmer's head.

Love in the Shine of Water

Dreaming at midday
— surprised and caught at it —
I've no excuses left.

None but the dry wind, say,
or napping to escape great heat.
But, Sir, the body's desert shifts.

Who is this thirst but me?
And what am I that I cry drink
enough to drown in: rivers,

lakes of it, whole seas,
where on that brink
I'll dive forever

into one green wave.
My landsman's weight
buoys up in raptures of the deep.

And as that diver craves
his deep-sea freight
such as the plunge, Love, if you should weep

Poor Thirst shall drink of tears,
and should your eyes
be green, what drinking's there

but the sea's colors,
the forest's rise
from single raindrops and the pouring air.

Landscape

The sun rises somewhere.
We cannot see it.
Here, houses shine in the cold air
and the sky is pewter.

Our streets glisten with rain
— None of your golden fat! —
The silver reflections
shake us again and again

and birds fall off their boughs
or turn, miraculous,
to crows. Everything goes
that isn't simplified enough,

reduced to lines on copper plates.
Nothing gold seduces us.
We claim by birthright
starkness as it is: black, white.

Theory of Games

With or without partners, we play at will.
Who claims these are the smallest victories?
Only the best men take the prizes home.
We know it. We feel it inside. Believe.
The bad hand, the spectacular good bluff
succeeds. There are no rules against winning.
Our frauds are only minor, after all,
part of the game. And we have kept these rules
down to a science. There are conventions,
responses. We seldom lose a hand.
Occasionally there is this desire
to stop and have it over and done with.
Some men admire our skill and dexterity
although they complain about content,
ultimate purpose. A game is a game.
We can play games without being masters.

The Puzzle

This is a puzzle, Love,
broken and in pieces.
We put it together,
so, making a picture
we have never seen,
something wholly imagined.
Between us on the table
are these thousands of pieces
mostly of one color: green.
We shall build forests,
long careful lawns
sloping down to the sea.
Waves are breaking.
Skies of great clouds,
dramatic, benevolent,
grow in these rich countries
only now revealing themselves,
here, under our fingers.
Whose is this world?
We put it together,
so, making a picture,
a dependent landscape.
Even so the great house —
necessary to these formal
plantings and prunings,
these prearranged mazes
ending nowhere but among
themselves — rises beyond
the range of our vision.
We need not enter that decay.
But where are the watchmen,
the masterful watchmen?
We suspect they hover, alert
in the depths of the garden
watching our waiting, though surely
we grow at this distance hard
to decipher, impossible to protect
as we dissolve like phantasy

into twilight and dense fog.
Now our improbable fingers
plunge down from this puzzling,
momentary hesitation to fill
the dark space in the bushes
where the unplanned, unsought-for,
gathers itself to happen.

The Trunk

How cool it is in the attic.
We open the remaining trunk.
Folded on top is a blanket,
blue, filling the top of the trunk.

Removing it we discover
flowers, a blanket of flowers
lying on sheets of white paper
oiled with the shape of flowers.

And beneath, another blanket,
red this time, thick for a winter
of much snow, and under it,
flowers, pressed from the winter.

More and more layers, secrets
discovered, down to the bottom,
or nearly, flowers, blankets,
secrets, and there at the bottom

a dog, wrapped against winter,
dead among the thick blankets,
red furred, pet of the strangers
who left the trunk, flowers, blankets,

the dog, here in our attic
for us, for us with the trunk
replacing flowers, blankets,
closing the lid of the trunk.

Root to Branch

What lives so close to roots has needs
dark and demanding. These burrows,
tunnels, nests, end in blind alleys.
Who hides, what creatures stir, what hunts
are darkly conducted, won, lost,
struggled for, end in conjecture.
The surprised whimpers, enemies unseen
but confronted, disturb our sleep.
We dream high up in the branches,
desiring air and the daylight.
We choose never to come down
into such stealth, such treachery
as feeds on darkness. Daylight
hits us all the same: dead center.

Diabolus in Musica

He marvels at his wrists, his fingers.
What matters is of course the music.
The piano is hidden from us,
played in secret from the second floor.
No one here is admittedly jealous.
What we have learned, mostly, is to listen,
to demand purity by never looking.
We insist: the pianist's the ghost of himself,
the chromatic fantasy. We marvel
at what matters of course, the music,
the intended surface. Look! That lover
who brings orchids plans an assault.

For Jonathan

Your friend Don, Jonathan,
discovered in the road
two green lights shining.
A black cat teetered
to death on the asphalt.
Don gunned it and drove on —
Some things can't ever be helped.

Today he remembers
the eyes of the cat
— brilliant and lucid —
its bagful of broken bones
held in the unbearable texture,
the soft fine household
of its perfect fur.

Small Pieces for a Big Mosaic

1
How the rooster,
iridescent in its dung,
strutting the henhouse rafter,
shakes feather over egg and hen,
barrels up his lungs,
swallows them and then
hysterically squawks to dawn
the love he croaks and feeds upon.

2
Once we are out from the slap of the tide
and our boat rides on the shell of the sea,
see how the sea holds land on every side
like cradle or crib. And how to me,

caught up in a manner of flesh speaking,
your arms are soft and strong by what they keep:
surface alive like a dark sea breaking
and underneath immovable for deep.

3
Leda, for all I know,
may well have loved
that damnable, insistent swan;
and if she turned field to that white plow
we make so much of,
who will blame her? At least she shows
she knew a thing or two
of man.

4
I would make you idle like some beast,
torpid with winter fat, sleek and slow,
let you brood alone and then feast
on your own substance in the cold snow,

and after storms had caught and packed you in,

starved you lean, I'd come after all, spill
fresh blood on places where you had been,
draw you out and stalk you and then kill.

5
How any fish,
who breeds no warmth inside him
but the sea's and that small stash
of sperm with which he seeds his fry,
still touches his dim
ladies till he dies.
And though he coldly mate
the number of his fry is great.

For the Fattened Flocks

Straight from the razor
the long-haired rams
bleat out their rage
at being newly shorn.
And gathered to that some-time
shaver, now their shepherd,
they graze about us,
vacant, absent-minded.
Praise to those placid heads,
the great skulls cropping grass,
the slow and stupid rise
of all their lordly horns
as, catching windward cries
of slaughter, the scent of wool,
they browse benevolent in stubble,
stony at the blood of lambs.

From the Mountain

If you can come this weekend
I'll meet you at the foot
of the mountain. Please send
your luggage on ahead by truck —
we cannot carry it.
The trail is steeper than the road
but more direct.
We'll climb it if the weather holds.

Bring boots. The rocks are sharper
than you'd think, although I hike
to town twice monthly and have neighbors
who visit in the spring and fall.
The rocks are covered up with snakes
who sit perfectly still
and never bite, but bloat and swell.
They bother only what they swallow whole.

Nothing is dangerous if you keep your head.
Only the weather is predictable.
My nearest neighbor once went mad
in a month of rain and killed his wife.
His only merit was he loved her well
and loves her still. I see him often
and he keeps his life.
He never visits when it forecasts rain.

I promise nothing.
I thought I heard you call me yesterday
and ran to meet you. The spring
is treacherous that way, a haze
hung over the willow grove. You ran away.
The threat of rain distracts me —
signs promise that it breaks today
and you are climbing up to me.

My Uncle Casts Stones for His Three Children

You scale a stone into the calm river
and the fish frighten off to deep water.

In my family only you are brilliant.
Yours is a strange, well-lighted world.
Stones drop from your hand: anger to darkness.

Gentlest of my uncles, your love flashes
the threatening promise, quick as disaster.

Testament

You brought it up
and asked my verse
be pared, be sparse.
I have not dared.
Such things are hard,
and will not blur,
nor be unsure,
nor cover up.

Letter to London

Dear woman, you write
how our city, Boston,
warms you in recollection.

And I recall your love
of walking in sundowns;
your pleasure at those
thousands of small, neat windows
along Beacon Street
— their long gold flash
at the last possible moment
of the sun's descent.
How those Colonial houses,
their red bricks, shone
for the whole October
of your going away.

After my own departure
I return in winter.
Soot befouls the snow;
London is as cold to you
as this is to me — these windows
blankly turning upward,
leaning to a leaden sky.
Memory cannot defeat them.
Think how we could stand
in one place only,
in the imagination;
how we were always leaving
as if we belonged somewhere
and among other people,
the late first choices
whom we left to find.

Statuary

She gives her child her left breast;
in her right arm, the child,
its eyes closed, sucks at her heart.
One imagines them as being alive,
the mother indeed merciful,
the child truly asleep, contented.
In their embrace is a gesture,
a heaviness in the arm,
a tension almost perceived,
weary of resurrections, visions,
continuations.
The mother appears to be listening,
hearing the wind hurry after itself,
the trees bending, birds flying westward,
crying Beloved, Beloved.

Motives

The rain falls
and this is a place of meeting.

The clouds move
and they have an ending in mind,

a far place,
a passion for confrontations.

The children,
running home from school in the rain,

remember.
And lovers also coming back

have reasons.
A man in a raincoat joins them,

his purpose
certain and never forgotten.

Processions!
The rain, clouds, children going home,

the lovers
rushing for cover from the rain,

the dark man —
hurrying to appointed hours,

promises,
doors, incredible reunions.

Ceremonial Entry

The glorious dome in the distance
shines in the klieglights.
Statesmen are somewhere within.
And there also, high up,
the Greek faces of statesmen
crowd the inner shell of the dome.
Someone cries out
"Immaculate! Immaculate!"
The intricately suspended dome
rings out with the cry.

From our outlying homes
the dome is visible
only in spring, the late autumn.
Beneath shade trees,
broad, especially planted,
we turn toward the capitol.
In the heat of summer
the prospect of the great dome
blurs like a mirage of water
uncertain now in the haze
but shining.

Lately there have been too many parades,
funerals, occasions of state.
The promise of greatness
is issued at intervals
from the halls of the rotunda.
And the rumors of assassination
filter down like leaves
without number or remedy
from a fabulous autumn.
But somewhere deep in the official halls
statesmen legislate
the ease of our sleep,
and politicians,
busy with codes and committees,
carry messages from the floor

of an irreproachable Senate.
We imagine them garbled.

We grieve deeply
and return to the suburbs,
waiting for autumn,
the clear vision of the dome,
how it rises over the favored,
spectacular change of the maple.

Now in the summer heat
we recall the vast acreage of the dome,
the silence, the clear whispers.
Visitors remember the coolness,
the precision and patience of guards
who answer all questions,
including the names
of the statesmen
carved high up on the rail
of the great balcony.
And if the shade of the dome
covers the excitement of public business,
for now the Greek faces of statesmen,
the concerns of their watching,
seem much the same to us.
We cannot recognize one from the other.

In the middle of summer
the memory of the high cold air of the dome
is never enough, never enough,
and we sit in the shade
waiting for the colorful change of the maple,
the red streets of the suburbs.

And now as one man,
like the first cold wind through the trees
murmurs of winter, of autumn,
we leave our homes
and the homes of our neighbors,
walking into the streets littered now with leaves.

The great bronze doors of the capitol
fling wide, open out onto the highways,
the sudden chill of autumn,
the sound of our walking,
our continuous arrival.
The floor of the rotunda
is filling with leaves,
the red leaves of the maple.
Someone is coming to greet us.
The floor has been washed,
swept clean,
each stone polished by hand.
They are pure white,
immaculate.
We may enter in.

THE INHABITED SCROLL

The Inhabited Scroll

As Leonardo once sent out
His perfect free-hand circled proof
Of mastery, myself have these 180
Thin degrees and one tree only.
Where you have seen my oak in spring,
The sun behind, both
Flourishing and green, the lawn
Before, the hill, the grass,
There is, had you gone round
About the other side, another
Side to everything:
Cliché and truth.

There on the sunstruck side so far
Unseen, inhabited and bare
Of leaves, I've carved such
Faces, familiar and farflung,
As will inhabit me, as well
Dear Quaker quaking at our core,
Peaceful, tyrannical, as well as thee.
One half my graven tree
Parades the public failure
Of all peace; the rest,
The grim, glad satisfactions
In domestic tyrannies.

But grand like the procession
Of whales, a sea of angels,
Pacific and salt, peer at us
Behind their scrollwork of leaves.
Resurrections of a billion fathers,
Mothers and the awkward children, picnics,
Confetti, coffins like small
Personal arks, sail past us.
And nothing of God but the sun
Who shines full-face upon them,
Making among the golden wooden leaves
Shadows and a greater dark.

One half the tree seems nothing,
Artifice; the other never to meet
Nor match the rest. One part, green,
Overgrows and overshadows
Everything; one, white wood
And worn, cut by my hand,
Corrodes and blanches out,
At last, in mystery. Figures,
Fables, one hundred thousand
Million leaves have yet to close,
Quite perfectly, the circle up
Into the reasonable, the just finality.

Poem for the Girl Who Would Bear Flowers into the New World like Bullets

You have asked me
To become a flower.
I know only one way
To do it
So that you'll remember
And never forget.
Therefore I lie here
With my one small paring knife
Newly sharpened,
With my dental drill
Saying "Watch.
This is for you."

Thus I cut slowly my face
Into two delicate parts,
Folding aside the flaps
Like blossoms,
Like Origami,
Great paper sails or wings.
I remove the eyes.
They burn like onyx
Or black bees
On their cushion of raw flesh.
I wish they were the favored
Color of blue.
You would prefer it.
But this will do.
This is exciting.

Now with the drill
I saw through the translucent
Shell of the skull.
And, behold, here is my mind,
Grey like the hardest stone,
But softer than water,
Cold, too, and quite dull
Next to the rainbow

Within me
I have yet to reveal.

For beneath my divisible chest,
Erupts from the flexible cage of my ribs,
Comes clamoring,
The heart, bursting for freedom.
Beside this the lungs
Ballooned with the world's air.
I will spread them apart
Carefully for you
And they will cover the whole earth.

Stomach, bowels, then,
The beautiful green jewel of the spleen.
Arms separated, pinned down,
These blue veins and their arteries,
Fall over my muscles
Like petals.
And the legs the same.
I am nearly a fan now.
So carried away am I
In this meticulous business at hand
Pain has no consequence.
This is for love.

Lastly I've saved
My wide yellow bladder
And the genital
Which divides like a drooping flag.
My testicles fall down like pearls
Into your hands.

And I have done it!
I am a flower
Round and with petals,
Colorful, vibrating.
I have done this for you
Much as you asked.
Now also you must do something for me,

Like put me together
Or just stand back and admire.
But whatever you decide
It will take a long time.

Simply to Say

You may not know this, Friend,
But the stars came out today
In broad daylight.
It was wonderfully exaggerated.
And someone kissed me
Who promised never to do it again.
I was enormously satisfied
And love myself
A bit more now than yesterday.
That was nice of you to do.
So I am writing this down
To hand you when you leave
Or come back
Or stand still just as you are,
Merely to say how simple it is to say
"Look! How you have pleased me"
And "Thank you"
And "Next to myself, Love,
You."

Mistress Bradford before Plymouth

Safe harbor. Landfall, you say — shipwreck
I call it. Disaster.
Sand and scrubby little bushes,
Savages in rotting furs.
If this be God's good luck
I break the same on human wishes.

Occasions of death
Work at us daily. There are none
Escape it. This piety, this seasick refuge
Hangs over me like a foul breath
Whose promises broken, one by one,
Unfasten thus in wreckage.

Who would pretend to understand
How much they truly lose
The things they leave?
Although I know, God pity us and save,
We do. I still refuse
Your newer England.

This is a man's business,
The killing to come, the carving out —
God's vengeance, and wilderness
Enough inside and out. I doubt
The homes we make outlast the woods —
The husbandries you keep will need these brides.

I swear I never chose this life,
This winter coming, this frozen
Harvest. God forgive us. Sir, adept
At failure, if you will, Lot's wife
I choose to look away and turn
And not accept.

Note: Mistress Bradford, the first supposed suicide of the new world, disappeared overboard from a ship anchored in calm waters within the harbor of the Massachusetts cape.

Sleeping in the World at Midnight and with Music

I dreamed how in a great asylum
So baroque as to be filled with
Music daily, I was Schumann.

How beside me, strict as nurses
But compassionate as saints
And wise as doctors, were my calm wife,

Clara, and the portly Brahms.
They played together on two twin pianos
While, in an interval of casement windows,

I saw such inmates as could walk were
Walking slowly to the stately music,
Upright, awake, and nearly conscious.

And I dreamed I wrote a spring cantata,
Then fell asleep to hear it sung
By thousands to a background faintly

Reminiscent of two clear pianos.
Within the room there was a globe
Of all the world which I kept turning,

Rhythmically, to match the stepping of those endless patients.
I rose to give a courtly smile to Clara,
Shake the hand of Brahms in friendship,

And withdrew to stroll upon the cushioned
Lawn with these, my brothers.
Beneath my feet I heard the world fall

Forward into traffic; behind me
There was music of my own
That I remembered. And I knew that here

I was poor Schumann and poor Schumann
Only, once musician, now the harmless madman
Of one room that, spinning, kept the world before him.

After Genesis

I am building an Ark,
Not after the measurements
Of the Lord,
But after my own.
It would be large enough for me,
A few friends,
All the beasts of the field.

Daily, though I'm no Noah,
My neighbors put on
The shifty glance of the paranoid —
Their suburban idea
Of suspicion somehow perfected.
They know I know something,
But no word escapes me
Save the rippling soft laughter
Which falls out of me
Like rain beginning.

Already my Ark
Has risen over the roofs of their houses.
Secretly, by night,
I dance gleeful and naked,
Covered with pitch
And the odor of hardwood.
Off-hours how I have skulked about
Repeating to myself
Two of these, and, of those, two more.
By midnight I steal them blind.
Their pets are disappearing
Like sugar into the mouth of the Mississippi.

Into my great red-ribbed wood ship
I have built a barnyard,
An unbelievable zoo.
Nothing can stop the stowed-in beasts
From their delight
In themselves, their knowledge

Of multiplication.
Who could keep up with it?
No one but me
Believes in the billowing rain,
The need for discretion,
The manageable size.

Yet walking the darkening streets,
My admiration for beautiful specimens
Like yourselves,
Your dancing by twos,
Has no sense of proportion.
I wish to leave behind me
None of you.
You have smiles not even the whole earth,
Prostrate in mourning,
May equal.

For you, then, I am rebuilding
My Ark according to the proportions
Of my desires.
Not even the Lord
Could imagine such love,
Such need,
Such passion for the number two.
Not even the rains of Noah
Nor the tears of God
Falling forever
Could float the city
My boat has become at last
For the sake of you.

Bestiary: Goat

Yesterday I decided
To become a goat
And when I woke this morning

I had two hooves,
Tufts of hair all over the place,
And one tail.

So I said to myself
"Just what you asked for"
And began to think, immediately,

Sex.
I was inordinately preoccupied
And that's the way

My day went —
All 24 hours of it.
But whenever I met someone

I thought fence, tin cans,
Erotica everywhere and
They thought goat.

So I'm beginning to think,
After all,
It wasn't worth it.

So tomorrow I'll be a gorilla.
They live in trees
And birds don't care

What you look like
And you don't care
They don't care, either,

So long as they keep singing.

Bestiary: Giraffe

I want to be a giraffe
So I can see farther than anybody
And eat leaves
Off the tops of the most elaborate trees.
Someone told me those are sweetest.
I would be greedy beyond belief
And no one could care
For even in the middle of famine
Giraffes don't eat their friends
As lions do
But browse in the pastures of green trees,
Great tottering monuments.
And the lions know
How even with my head in the air
I could be brought low.
So with my huge long legs
And luck
I could gallop away,
Although if cornered at last
I, of all the animals,
Would not bow down to my enemies.
Giraffes aren't built that way.

We Have Come Back

Observe — defenses
Of my fists, my heart —
The black and flooding sea,
The sullen houses
We at one time fled
And gratefully.

We have come back —
No more, no less than that —
Into a past we keep
Inquisitorially suppressed
As if what's there were also black
And criminally deep.

What of those charitable faces
And relinquished livelihoods?
When we in turn let go
When first we must, and could,
What meaning's there?
What strength? What good?

Still we return.
And what we might have loved
But learned to hate
And then dismiss, forget,
Comes orphaned toward us
Beckoning but late.

Observe — defenses
Of my fists, my heart —
How willfully we do not care.
Dear past, if you were loveless
I am cruel. You cannot change
Nor I repair.

What then have I come for
But to see in your thin lips
And in your scornful eyes

50

The first cold landscape I refused?
As in those places I have lately run to
It is you I recognize.

Where We Have Traveled in Our Dreams

1.   Sometimes also
I have dreamed
Judiciously.
As on calm waters
I have drifted homeward
As you too have done,
Into shore, sunlight,
The outstretched arms
Of our fellow countrymen.
And I have found
The slow sea journey
Boring, the citizens
Unworthy of my love.
And when at last I then
Debarked from sleep
I then pronounced
The nighttimes useless
And our shared days the same,
The stony suburbs,
The subways endless
And arriving always
At a destination
We — last year, this year —
Sorrowfully predicted.
And I have hoped then
For an end to dreaming
And an end to hope.

2.   But there are times
When all my dreams
Seem bitter as years,
The years as storms
Falling one on one:
Waves on this shore
Where flimsy houses
Huddle up together.
And feeling in danger
Of death, faring farewell

My friends, my family,
I begin to drown
And terribly swim
To the ports of daylight,
The noises and traffic
Of morning. And living
With the faint, sweet
Echo of my death
My days become dark
With calamities,
Breakages so vast
I see them nowhere
But in the sea's arms.
And I have turned
To hope as a kind
Of swimming and then
To my pillow
And such dreams
As shook me
And so greatly mattered.

Poem for a Summer Birth

For Mark Rettig

Child, this is a celebration
Not of your birth
Which comes no more
But of the name you, henceforth,
Live with and shall answer to.

You bear a kinship
To all things Venetian:
Those two great rivals of clarity,
Water and glass;
To one princely cathedral
And, of the same name, her square
Proud of an ancient commerce,
Idlers, tourists, pigeons,
All things pedestrian
Which linger there
And pass on.

And you are bound forever

To the pen,
To what you put on paper
And never erase;
As also, inescapably,
To those deeds where we shall meet
And know you
For you will burn in your lifetime
The fearful, indelible mark
Of yourself.

And you are bound at last
To the Mark of hope,
His chronicles of paradise
Which for your sake
I shall call promise,
Whom I echo

Celebrating yourself,
Your arrival into a world
Already carrying your name
Like a banner:
"Be of good comfort, rise;
We calleth thee."

From the Color of the Olive Leaves, Which Is Silver...

The snows have shapes
Unending; the rains
One drop, again
And again the same.
Great cold has means
To take what warmth
May yet remain,
Like art cut out
The liquid part
Into the frozen
Shine of an immense
Complexity.
Throw out the sea
Into the sky
And, instantly,
That sea grows cold
Like fractured diamonds
Hanging orbit
In the void,
Forever still
But turning yet
Between a zero absolute
And incandescences
Of stars and sun.
And Physics says it.

So we, like snow
And rain, contain
Such hidden roots,
The darkly measured
And elaborately
Still geometries
Of where we stand.
Our passion
Runs like water
On the granite
Or absorbent ground
Which holds us up

While we ourselves
Cannot hold still.
Then death (which comes
We know like cold,
Or snow, or winter,
Or the end of us)
Says Here. Now. Thus.
And swift as knives
Into the heart,
Like broken lungs
And minds adrift,
Farewell, we loved you.
Like grass which grew
And bended for one time
Together but turns
To an imaginary
Winter wheat of ices,
Or the silver pallor
Of the olive leaves,
We have stopped stock-still
As stone stops, absolute,
The movement ended,
Though we turn and turn
And know not of it.

Welcomed into Foreign Rooms

Since some of us are always
Sitting together, we do so
By observing the ceremonial
Placement of chairs and sofas.
In some measure we become
What our host in the abstract
Imagines his guests to be
When they are not apart.
Though the design constricts us
We are seldom more precise
Than our surroundings.
Small wonder a man
Lays down his possessions
In an arrangement
Unmistakably his own.
Think of our host's loneliness
When his guests are gone,
Each room, each object
In each room an ordering
Against the furious weather
Of the world's silence.
Even now our emptied rooms
Wait to be filled perpetually.
Consider this the greeting
Of one man to another.

HOLY ORDERS

ANIMALS

Crowing

Rooster,
Iridescent in his dung,
Struts the henhouse rafter,
Shakes feather over egg and hen,
Barrels up his lungs,
Swallows them and then
Hysterically squawks to dawn
The love he croaks and feeds upon.

Swan Song

Leda, for all I know,
May well have loved
That damnable, insistent swan;
If she turned field to that white plow
We make so much of,
Who will blame her? At least she shows
She knew a thing or two
Of man.

Breeding

Fish,
Who breeds no warmth inside him
But the sea's and that small stash
Of sperm with which he seeds his fry,
Still touches his dim
Ladies till he dies.
And though he coldly mate
The number of his fry is great.

Torturing Toads

Boys go to toads
Because they hop
On land and stop

To be plucked up.
We caught a toad
And on a board

We nailed him flat.
With lighter fluid,
A match, we stood

And watched him burn.
He had gold eyes
And liquid tears.

He turned to smoke
And ash and stick.
Well, boys are quick.

I tell you this:
I killed a toad
But not the world.

It wasn't much,
A little thing,
A slow burning.

For his gold eyes
No words at all
But gate to wall.

He looked without
And got within
A pin stuck in,

Deep in the eye,
Hard in the bone,
And leaped to stone.

Buck Fever

Good buck sports ten
Good points. Hunter trusts
His aim comes true

And doesn't lame
But cracks the heart
At once, as all

Good hunters do. The
Poacher's mercy blinds
Before he kills

And buck in that blind
Light falls massively
Down into night.

Some hunters stay
Their guns and do
Not shoot but stare

At buck as buck
Stares back, and freeze.
All three, an old

November tale
Of cold and buck
And hunter who please

To take and do
Not take and take
The breath away.

Medieval Tapestry: Animals Running

Two lions, a hound
And a hare
Hurry down an alley of grass.

The lions pound on
Hunting food.
They are not our villains.

Hound, the fever of
Sportsmen, snares
A scent. He has his teachers.

Hare wants to be chased.
Lions and hound
Split up his heart three ways

And eat so they
May sleep — two Holy
Lions, Brother Hound, Saint Hare.

Camels, Caravans, and Myth

I've bought a fleet
Of six camels
And am leaving town
As conspicuously as I can.
A wonderful way to get even.

This is the best of all ways
To say you have used me
And I'm going
Like the Grand March from Aida
Minus elephants.

Behind me
Break waves of sofas,
Double beds, moveable kitchens.
Back of each window
I spy white ties,
Gowned and smiling women,
Jeroboams of champagne,
The toast of my progress.

I rock on crying,
"Farewell, Farewell, Love me,
"I have done my best.
"Not even the tears in my eyes
"Can match the price
"Of your extravagant notice."

Whereat I say to my cat Hodge,
"This is the end of something."
Which to her means nothing at all.
But camels know.
We've twelve days without water
And leave this historic place
Full up to here
With water and fat.

When the dreamy opera's over,
Hodge purrs under the stationary
Sofa. I'm home with the double
Bed, the desk and the kitchen.
Everything's nailed flat to the floor.
Love can stick on the lips
Like tar and shingles, not even
The roof will leak rain.

The world's comfortable desert
Kills camels, keeps cats, purrs
What the telephone pressed to
Our ear promised: voices, connections,
Wonderful ways to get even,
Electric farewells, hellos,
Alases, etceteras.

Camels are for men and women
Who crawl through divorces and
Alcohol, not dry crackers and
Breadcrumbs. Sand sings
And sometimes we hear it.

GODS

For Holy Mother Church

You are the mother
Of castrati, those ball-less
Wonders. You are the

Choirs that held them.
Only the angels have
Voices so purely cold.

Or so they say who say
They know. Nowadays
Counter-tenors must make

Do. Sopranos, in a pinch,
Have done wonders
Musically. Even a friend

Of miraculous virtue, a
Woman, insists Christ
Comes out effeminate.

I, Dear Mother, am naturally
Different. What's cut from me
Gets no permission. All the same,

High notes cut clean. Christ
In his habit rises in fire
And flowers from acres of ice,

A triumph of clear-cut
Contempt. Mother, I am
Your own good son.

I am the master of my own
Two balls. I am
The king of winter.

The Return

I am coming home
Like the cows,
With bells on

Shouting "Grandpa,
"I love you"
And "Grandma,

"I love you."
We're all a little bit crazy
But not many of us

Can live it the way you do,
So completely, carrying it
Right into the pasture

And beyond.
Hoeing potatoes, Grandpa,
And, See, here they are again

Your fiery angels
Calling out with voices like bells,
Cowbells, "Hurrah, Hurrah."

Grandma,
Milking in her wedding dress,
Dances at midnight

That same way
And with nobody —
But it was a waltz

And that takes two.
Years later I'm here,
An assortment of wicked lovers

(though they were beautiful)
To show for myself,

And myself

Which is worse yet.
Well, thinking about you,
Now and again, like this,

Is a great relief
Because, ah, the style you had
And I'm envious.

So I almost believe
I'm home, really, like the cows
And with bells on,

Clanging "Hello, Goodbye, Goodbye,
"My two good fools"
And no one,

Not even myself,
Can take you away.

Uncle Roy

At the time of his death
Nothing happened.

Across the Rockies
Aunt Linda was off

To one more hobby fair.
"Life is a joke,"

She said,
Los Angeles proves it.

"Boy," Roy said,
"Your Grandmother's

"Already in heaven."
I knew better.

She was in Canada.
Good Baby Jesus

Gave her Christmas
Every single day.

I was in school
When he died.

Bells were ringing
And my brain went black

As the bore
Of a cannon.

I roared.
By God! Nations surrendered,

Multitudes.
Don't tell me

I don't know death.
I believe in it.

The Extermination of the Jews

Not just that Sarah
Will never shut up and talks,
Talks, talks
In her sleep, through mine,
Through everything.
But, God, the fantasy
Of just me shutting her up
Once
And for all.

Because Harvey writes
Better poems than I do.
He can't help it.
So God should take care of
Me better than this
Since I'm a Catholic besides
And he isn't.
And I'm thinking.

Because Saul, my butcher,
Sold me a bad chicken
The day before he shot himself,
And I can't reach him there.

Because Robert
You're the brother I never had.
I'm wishing I could have wiped
Just once your bloody nose,
Picked you up from under the tree
You climbed and fell from,
Your arm broken.

Because, Christ,
We are cleverest
Getting rid
Of the ones we love
Or who teach us.

The Wings of Angels

The wings of angels
Are not gold.

They weigh heavy
As the feathers

Of pigeons.
Primitive old

Masters paint
Annunciations.

Mary, a marvel
Of good sense,

Surrenders always
To their miracle.

Like a wife
Peeling an onion

She has completed
A good deed and

Said hello graciously.
In antique

Crucifixions,
Christ on a

Cross of courtesies
Collapses in

Serene good taste.
Above on their wings

Angels fly
Hallelujahs of horror.

Thank God! I am hummed
To sleep by engines

And water faucets.
Common sense

Consoles me, like a
Good wife she

Turns down my sheets
Onto a clean bed.

Glad am I she
Isn't truthful

As the wings of angels
Which slam shut

Like iron beds
And the narrow

Doors of
Devastating stone.

Doors

Valentine
Out for a stroll
Hears the clapping of hands
Everywhere.

Supermarket
Doors sweep open
Before him. His hands have
Nothing to do.

When he jumps
Up and down on
Their threshold, doors flap
Applause.

In revolving
Doors, all he misses
Are horses and chariots;
Carousel

Music he hums
Through his teeth.
He goes round and round, dancing
With others.

Moveable
Stairs escalate
Him higher and higher. With no
Thought at all,

Valentine
Becomes more noble,
More elevated.
Elevators

Swoosh him
Down into sunlight
And a first-floor of highways

And laughter.

He runs ten miles
To his room. He weeps,
Hazzahs for the love
The world gives up

To him freely.
Then Sunday. The magic
Doors lock shut in his face.
He wishes hard.

But the stairs
Move not one inch upward,
Never mind to heaven. Besides,
It is raining.

Driving Truck

I want us driving
A truck. We haul on roads
Cleverer than the

Snakes in Eden. They
Think we are Adam
And Eve. They say to

Us, "Eat, dream, drive. Roads
"Are wonders." You tell me,
"Drive trucks, yourself, Friend.

"Eat crow. Fly like the
"Crow." Buddy, I just
Drive forever in

Circles. Crows fly round
And round, too. You never
Noticed. Even the

Earth isn't straight and
People live around corners.
Trucks in a mystery

Bear anything anywhere.
Try that on schedule.
Carry treasure for

Somebody else. At
3 a.m. drive in
The dark. Jesus, there's

A journey. We get
Where we're going and
Strangers unload beds,

Baby's booties, food,
A thousand wholesale

Suits and dresses. All

Empty and 4 a.m.
And all alone, Buddy,
We're driving on back.

Ask snakes. Ask Columbus.
The world's not square.
Drive straight on

In circles. Drive a
Truck. Drive. Carry. Go
To God. Roads are wonders.

PEOPLE

The Yes We Say

It's "Yes" we whisper when we dare not go.
We stay. We think it is an act of will.
Time in the long run only can say "No."

Though boys and girls make love in beds of snow
And kill with kisses ice, but not its thrill,
The "Yes" they whisper means they dare not go.

When wives and husbands in the night both know
Their last cold quarrel feeds on deeper chill,
Time in the long run only can say "No."

In bars when men and women row on row
Eye sex as sex, then just the same, glacial's
The "Yes" they whisper when they nod and go.

A fifth-floor stranger's face may mean to throw
Heart, head away, but grab the windowsill.
Time in the long run can only say "No."

Poor Jacks and Jills, however fast or slow,
They'll lie down breathless underneath the hill
With "Yes" or "Whisper" or "We dare not go";
Time in the long run can only say "No."

Valentine to An Arsonist

You must be secret
And as common as grass.
We pass you by day
But never know you.

Like the Nazis
In hiding, anonymous
As my Uncle Bill,
I miss everywhere

Your face, imagine
Here at my front door,
You, defying description,
The police, lighting a match.

A student whom I
Never taught died two
Nights ago two streets
Away. A neighbor whom

I never met I will not
Meet at all. But you are
Staying safely with someone
Somewhere among us,

A ferocious, portable
Accident, capable of
Inventive Aristotelian
Logic, pets, good friends,

Laughter. Let us be
Honest with each other;
We will find you out;
You need us.

Like a lover you come
At night to surprise us,
And we are so many,

So various.

Our sheer number
Exhausts you; you
Cannot escape it.
Listen. You're burning alive.

History Lesson

My friend, the poet,
Writes in the countryside.
He says I should join him.

My friend, the young teacher,
Teaches
And loves his students.
He teaches me about love.

Even an old teacher tells a friend
How I could be eccentric
To some good purpose.
If only I loved myself.

Meanwhile he is on his third wife
And I am always falling
Asleep in his living room.

My friend in the country
Writes poems
And pays his bills.
He is a good neighbor.

The students of my friend
The teacher
Teach love.
They are not famous.

The countryside
Of my friend the poet
Is not famous.

My friend, the old teacher,
Has a kind of fame.
He puts me to sleep.

From That Sleep of Exhaustion There Is No Awakening

Death,
When I think of you,
You are my neighbor's son,
The boy next door,
All swagger
And the smell of perversion.

You have trespassed down our walk
Since I can ever remember,
Kissed the cheeks of my aunt
In her twenties.
She swooned in a fever.
She married you.
My sister ran into your
Promise, gasping,
Her eyes wide open.

How you are young,
Handsome,
Infuriating.
We look away
And you smile.

When I come to my door,
You are climbing the porch,
Hands extended,
Sweaty and murderous.
I turn away
As if I love you secretly,

As if some day,
Taking your hand,
I am your husband forever,

Will jump up like the passive wife
Throwing confetti
After the complete coitus,
When your hair will be

Perfume, perfection,
Everything scandalous.

And I will sleep with you
Forever, forever

Faithful while you go
Elsewhere, jumping the fence
To every new back yard
Where we are sitting, feverish
In the early evening,
Waiting for you, too,
To, once and for all,
Come
And amaze us.

In the Closet

I have been living
Here in the closet
Smothered by last

Year's sweaters, with
The sweet, white
Corpses of moths.

When someone coughs
At the keyhole, I rise,
If I rise, like stars.

They peer at my navel.
I do not know if they
See some singular

Well without water
Or the last, visible
Sign of my birth.

Perhaps they see an
Eye, hard, black, and
Unblinking: the look

Of a madman hunting
A target. I lie down.
The snow of moths

Drifts over me cold
As Canadian winters;
Their eyes burn red

As that ruby deep
In the heart called
Desire. I breathe a

Tight vinegar poison
That killed them, hot

In the furnace of ice.

I touch the honey and
Ashes of all who have
Loved him in shadows,

Here with the moths,
The dust and the wardrobe,
Dumb as a landscape.

Black Confetti

This morning I threw the plates, pots,
    And pictures up in the stale air
Of the living room. Not one came down.
    The furniture joined them.

I locked my door on the jubilation
    Of what I live with, a flying
Squadron of chairs and tables. I went
    To work a mystic and juggler.

When like an anchor I sat at my desk
    The air conditioner fanned at my face
Five dancing banners of white streamers.
    They never fell either, but flowed.

Joy was a merry-go-round with or
    Without me. When two dozen people
Asked me for staples before noon,
    A miracle shot from their feet.

They sailed like my flat china plates,
    The very pictures of that joy
Of white stars that never seem to fall,
    But in the great pan of the sky

Brave, one by one, the black confetti
    Of night-time, the apartments
We live in, the beds where while
    We sleep there we dream, only

To suffer the amazement of waking,
    And, tossing out our lives onto
The cold floor (but not for one
    Moment falling) we must juggle joy.

THE MAGIC SHOW

I

The Magic Show

We're all assembled for the magic act.
Children rustle in the first three rows.
Glamour's about to break the neck of fact.

We grown-ups, who understand such shows,
Huddle cheerfully far in the back
Although a little apprehension grows.

Confetti may shower down like golden flak
And our illusions might fly out of hand.
Faster-than-the-eye's no reassuring tack.

But the magician catapults his wand,
Parts the curtain, and—boisterous applause!—
Pours dry champagne from a carafe of sand.

An elephant floats buoyantly like gauze,
Becomes a cloud, then two, then sails off.
And we are smiling, all of us, whatever was.

The lady whom he elegantly saws in half
Vanishes stage right *and* left clean out of sight
Leaving behind a disheveled, disembodied laugh.

She reassembles in her rhinestone tights
And shimmers earthward from the flats above.
Then, out of his hat, he pulls a chip of light

Which flung now up in the air becomes a dove.
Our clapping shatters it to stars that move
Into each grown-up eye one tear for love
Whose loss, like magic, we are frightened of.

Midwinter

Cheerful Father O'Reilley
Warns me how you
God, cold, hard,
Right hand of the Universe,
Hide under my bed,
Peeking.

And since sometimes from my dead-
Drunk sleep I toss in a
Sunday hangover, who knows better
Than Thee how simple
My boring

Country pleasures,
How common the rusty
Creaks of my bed.
Who knows better than Thee

How warm that bed,
How cold the wind
In the shining space

Of the stars.
How February, that useless month,

Shortest in days, hangs on, hangs on.

The Three Rag-Pickers of Joy

In alley and in early dark
  They sort in a flutter
Of bills, bottles, old tin cans.

They read the lives of Joy Street.
  What were the wines, the red,
The white, my wealthy neighbors drank

Last night? What beer went stale?
  What flowers withered early
And got tossed? And why? The medicines

That spinned us groggily to bed
  Empty there, and empty, too,
The vials that plastered up our

Cracking heads. These they leave
  To take instead half-remembered
Tokens we'd counted on as trash.

Observe. Parts we easily tossed off
  Go well-regarded into strangers'
Hands. And see. Out of the picked

Bones of my day, out of the
  Barrel fat with bad news, comes
This poem to those who live on Joy

Street, salvaging from yesterday's
  Losses or memories or pains
A trifle we can carry home to sleep.

For Christ in His Triumphant Majesty

After the rain has fallen,
    After February freezes it
And the lady next door
    Who has been a 24-hour
364-days-of-the-year
    Bitch is kind and a lady
Since she needs a
    Ride to town and my wheels
Spin on the only highway out
    And the world needs a
Bastard as I am fast
    Becoming to come to terms
With it, then, when
    Everyone was shut up for once
Deep in their houses
    Yesterday, the sunlight shone
In the middle of the ice
    Hanging from the scraggly bushes
At the living room window
    Where the two cats keep looking,
For Christ knows anything
    That moves is proper game, and gives
Up today the living spark
    In the guts of winter which means
Christ, you are alive, have
    To be if the ice shines like fire
Yet . . .

Dick and Jane and Jubel and Me

Dick and Jane,
The almost-married couple
Down by the bog,
Need a ride to work.

Thus,
We are driving away,
Dick and Jane—
And me,

Who am the author
Of this little trip.
Off we go.
Jane's getting new work,

Dear, happy, merry Jane.
Dick puts trains
Together, a wonder,
And I like

That. I put
Nothing together.

But here we are
Going to work,
Dick, Jane, me
And I like them

Even when Jubel
Flat-footed over my
Flowers, that God-
Damned clod in the eye

Dog of Dick and Jane
Chases us down the road
Where I'm kidnapping—
So he thinks—

Dick of the thrown stick,
Jane, giver of food.
Yelping on air, Jubel
Limps home, so I chuckle

When Dick and Jane
Have a laugh of their own.
Ha! Ha! they say
Jubel once pissed

On the four posts
Of your property.
And I know what that
Means. Possession.

Dick, Jane, me—
And I like them.

St. Valentine's Day

The boy in the back
Of the class studies
The black hair and the
Thin wrist of the girl
He desires. He forgets
The assassination
His teacher recounts
Though the teacher's mind
Can keep dates straight while
Flashing on the face
He loves by night
And by day, the wife
Who sweeps on toward
The flat of her own
Lover who regrets
The inconvenience,
Expense, the sad lack
Of time. He checks his
Watch (for she is late).
Meanwhile his son drinks
Coffee in a diner
And dreams of a boy
He met last night in
A park and now loves.
He misses the waitress
Who serves him his cream.
She dreams of her two
Daughters. She wishes
They could live with her
And the woman she
Rooms with. She sighs and
Remembers her niece,
A girl with thin wrists
And a fondness for
A boy in the back
Of her history class,
And she would approve
That at that moment

He has just flushed out
First-love returned when
The girl turns and smiles
At him, her saint, his
Valentine, by God,
Their hearts on their sleeves,
The puppy lovers,
The adulterers, the gay,
The neat, the driven,
Burning a bit like
Light spilt from light on
The eyes of blind men
Cured too soon: terror
Not delight, then pain,
And then the bright, bright,
Bright Saint Valentine.

II

The Love Letters

You read the letters
Like a soldier
Studying the map
Of a ruined city.

This is the season
When love
Grows.

Nothing has fallen.
The chestnuts
Send up flowers
Like white torches.

You meet your friends
On the street.
Their greetings
Ring friendly
And metallic
Like the voices of critics.

Nothing has changed.

You grow pale
With loneliness.
You glow like a lamp.
No one notices.

Be good,
Be brave,
You tell yourself.
This is a new thing.

Under the lamp
You read the letters.
Like so many levers
They pry more deeply
Into love.

You become specific.
The phone does not ring.
Nor the doorbell.
No one visits.

You imagine
The face you desire.

You abandon
Images,
Turn the pictures
To the wall.
You love.

You go to bed
Believing an angel
Peers down
Through a crack in the ceiling.

You close your eyes
To avoid
The light.

You leave the lamp burning
In the living room
For love
Who comes home late.

You accept change.
You love.

You call it
Courage.

The Divorced House

The house lost
Half its heart.

The pets, off
In their separate

Places, curled
Up to mourn.

When birds sang,
The kitchen

Table was twice
Too big.

At night
Fewer lights went on,

The need
For electricity

Lessened,
And in the bedroom

While the traffic increased
There was less

True sleep.
Still, the mind

Of the house
Was no longer

Divided.
Each chair

Would have but
One master,

The pets
One set of commands.

In the attic,
Escape was

Easier—
Only one pair

Of hands
Would be laying

Traps.
Everywhere else,

With the impudence
Of a thrown-away kiss,

Tyranny
Came home.

Saying Goodbyes

After the divorce
The clean white sheets,
The blank second pillow
Shine like winter.
Pleased with yourself
You learn to lie alone.
All good things go on
Too long like this.
One day reproach
Like a blank page
Overwhelms you.
Something must be
Written, you say,
Even trouble, and you
Rumple the sheets
The way the lonely
Check for footsteps
In the virgin snow:
Someone may have come
Though no one was home,
Though no one could answer.
You invite stain,
Buy colored sheets,
And cast off mourning.
Now you can grieve
The good times past.
Which naturally surprises.
So you plan ahead.

Blond

I am not going to invite you,
For once, into my life.

Others may call you beautiful
Or handsome, but not from my lips

Any praises. This is the way
It should be with strangers,

Always. What if your hair be
The hair that shines bright in

Dark places? So does the sun
In the eye of the storm and,

O, we are just winds flying
About you. But not from my

Lips will you hear a sharp
Cry in the street—some summons

To follow. What if I dodge you
All night? Loiter behind you?

What matter? Off you go!
Home to your cloister of ciphers!

I will not praise you. I sprawl,
Instead, on a splendor of pillows.

In the late guttering light,
Tilted to sleep, I am biting my lips.

Going Blinded Home

And when at forty
Love began once more,
I felt as I once felt,
Head bent and huddled,
Trudging through the snow.
Why this surprise
When I have done it all,
Or so I thought, before?
Why one more sudden storm
To get through, when to go
Means leaning breathless
In the wind, the heart
Less steady, and the eyes
Turned upward, wet
And burning in the cold?
What else to do
Except to go the old
Way, blinded, home
Where one familiar door
Flies open to a table
Where my hunger's fed
When I have made it through.

Falling Asleep

Under my shoulder
You turn
To sleep.

In the slight twitch
Of an opened
Finger
I feel you
Slip
Like a gifted child
Into your private world.

Outside the window
All over October
The countryside
Drops
One by one
Gold leaves.

Locks turn.
Lights go out
In the respectable
White houses.

I know how men and women
Bolt their houses
Against thieves.

I cannot deny this.
I have heard their stories.

Everywhere
The world
Lets go.
I know.

I know
And tighten my arms

And catch you
Catching myself.

In the good night
Of a private act
I follow you.

Michael's Poem

Anything I can give you
You already
Possess.

I tell you this
Lie
To keep you

From adding up
More debt.

Nevertheless, stand near me.
I hold out
A gift

Palmed in the cup
Of my hand.

You must look close to even see it
And no painter can paint it
For nothing is here.

Nor must we pollute it
With metaphor
And make of it
A hollowed stone,
The bowl of a beggar.

Take it as it is:
A handful only of air,

An openhandedness,
A gesture
For you alone,

The most human
Of courtesies.

You understand such things,

How behind
This nothingness

That no one else
Ever will care for

Or, caring solely for you,
Ever will notice
Or steal,

How behind
A lightness
Even you cannot change
Or throw away,

Beneath what I hold in my hand,

Under this clarity,
This vacuum of the heart,

Cups the tight
Skin of my will

Where I begin.

The Breaking In

When he had fallen
In love the last time
And kept loving
What he'd loved before,
His heart broke once.
When he'd disappeared
Into love once too often,
This then was the puzzle:
Two goes into three
How many times?
Outside the spring
Astonished him as ever
And the birds flew
Back to his gardens
And flocked before him
Like pity descending.
He found himself reciting
Over and over again
A puzzle: three goes into two,
He thought, and saw
The flowers multiply
Like love gone wild.
One goes into one
Goes into one, he prayed,
When his mind shook,
When his heart revolved,
When in a house mullioned
With mirrors, he reflected
Only multiple landscapes
And he fell into love
Over and over and over.
Like an unfailing season
He floated toward summer
While his heart shot out
The bright, shining shards
Of all he reflected,
Of all he now loved
That threw him like a stone

Into the riots, the growths,
The flowerings, the springs.

III

The Extraction

More dubious than love,
You promise no pain.
Flat on my back, mapping
The blank white ceiling,
I feel the needle. "You must
Help me," you say. I numbly
Turn whichever way you ask.
True to your word, the wisdom
Teeth go with a sly sucking
Of bone from the clenched jaw.
Your brown eyes, closer
And clearer to me than any
One's straight gaze, shine
With sympathy and success.
"You did well." Now I am wise,
The good child, bright
And proud in the face of
The inevitable: What must go
Must go. I cooperate and,
Truly, there was no pain
At the pulling, no apologies,
No tedious explanations
About suffering. Walking to work
I think, "How easy," when the first
Throb of what is to come comes,
And I clutch in my pocket
Your prescription, the white
Paper with your signature
That drugs but will not stop
The needle of torn nerves,
The hard white nail in the bone
And the grey metal of pain
Ringing like a stunned bell
In the blue air of the brain.

Wearing My Alaskan Real Seal Parka

Just you watch me. I'm going
To wrap myself in seal skins,
Run around like an Eskimo
In polite, civilized places.
I'll wrap up, also, my friends.
My friends will open their mouths
Like fish, go gulp, gulp, gulp, poor
Life, poor living things, poor seals.
Poor deaths, divorces, and broken
Dishes, I might say, but I won't.
I'm too polite and I'm watching
Gossips, their curious kinship
With snipers—aiming, aiming.
Under our hot animal collars,
Synthetic or not, see how we
Pump up and down the corridors
Of live reputations. Like
Thermometers recording fevers,
Pestilence, we deliver the most
Exquisite post-mortems. Closer
To home we wrap ourselves in
Marriage, that sewed-up glory.
Don't get me wrong. I'm not against
Marriage, and killing offends me.
But bound in a seal's fur, you're
More handsome, more humble,
Wrapped in the lives of others.
Give me a world of lovers
And I'll shed skin, blood, furs,
For kisses, bedrooms and orgies,
Greeks and goats. But tell me
We have no furious hunger—
Even for beauty—and
You lie. Hunger means we must
Eat and chew up the living
And how it becomes us.

Flowers

These are the flowers of
Flowers, these are the flowers
Of women. We name them.

Marigold. Rose. Iris. The famed
Possessions of ladies, those vulgar,
Battering blossoms. The fine

Transparent flesh of the petal,
The gold and the Mary, think of it!
The soft, sweet hair at the lip

Of the Iris, that extravagance
Of gardens gathering the sweetness
Of women shamelessly upright

At the base of our hands, under
Our noses, that glorious doorway,
Herself, the world, profligate, bleeding.

Once More That Irrepressible Oh!

My students keep blossoming
In the most irrepressible
Shapes and sizes.
And the seizures, Oh, the seizures
Of the heart,
Oh, pretended, romantic excess.
Dear students,
May I kiss your hands,
Your knees,
The tips of your noses?

And you, my colleagues,
Dragging those pipes and tweeds
After you like tapestries,
Flappable, misplaced masterpieces,
And you, lovely ladies,
Crushing those PhD's
Under your low high-heels—
Oh, when you walk past my desk,
The office, electric and wanton,
Storms into the whorish,
Late, last flowers of August.

Give me, Oh, your minds,
Those winding stairs
To climb, my arms filled with
Your kisses, secret or
Public, the shame of it
All, as we say,
And I shall carry them
High up and throw out
The bouquets, bodies,
Colleagues, students, every
Last damned thing onto the bed
Of the world where we

Lie down together being
Lovers already loving or not.

Oh, Hurrah!

Walking in Maine

My father holds me up.
Across the room a window
Frames a picturesque
Cove, pine trees, a rundown
Waterfall breaking at the end
Of the Royal River. Yarmouth,
Maine, 1939. In front
Of the window my mother
Stands and opens her arms.
My father finally lets go.
Everything begins thus.
Somewhere someone lets go
And we begin to fall. In this
Poem my mother calls my name
To keep me from being pulled
To the ground. One small
Leg flies out and checks
The world's downward tug.
I teeter, my other leg holds,
And I move out and I walk.
Past my mother's arms, out
Through the window, down
Onto a wide, marble, meta-
Physical staircase, I descend
Into this polished Maine June
Edged with renovated wharves.
The first applause of my
Parents forgotten, I make
Up what it must have been like
To begin to stand upright
Trusting in love: to fall,
To balance it, to call such
Broken falling walking.
A tourist in the town
I was born in, I watch a dozen
New sailboats strain for the wind
To get going. And the cove,
Catch of a hundred cameras,

Takes up what the waterfall
Flings prettily into the sea:
The Royal River, the present
Tense working buoyantly
Over the pull of a father,
A mother, a baby lit
In the brown shadow
Back of an open window
Falling in gravity.

Burning the Willamette Valley

Today the farmers are
Altogether as one burning
The Valley. We are
Driving into the
Willamette the three
Of us talking up the past
Going North on Route 5
As we are with ash
In the air and smoke
Floating on the heart
Of summer SLOW FIELD
BURNING read the signs
The farm boys hold up
Flames at their feet
The sun a bright
Coal at the back of
The thick clouds the
Sheep grazing along
Placidly and Mom sings
Her sadder sweet song about
Love and Dad's laughter
Resurrects a bad joke
"Where have they gone
I wonder" he asks
"The good friends"
The brown stubble darkening
And we cannot see one
Foot ahead in the road
Although the air does clear
And there it is the cold
White snow of the highest
Mountain while behind
The fields burns a column
Of sharp incense a
Black whirlpool the end
Of the harvest the valley
We have passed through.

Mortal Blows

When the squirrel
Flew into my car's wheels
I heard a crack
Of Thanksgiving
Like walnuts breaking
In two sweet halves,
Sweet meat
Into my hands.
In the rear-view mirror
He skidded all one piece,
Soft fur and tail,
Off to the ditch,
The two clear eyes
Never closing.
The eyes of a family
Like the dead
Never shut by themselves.
They watch you board the bus
Leaving them all behind.
"How could you do this?"
Is what goes after you.

Two years later
I hit a fox at midnight.
A bat hit a ball,
I thought, and stopped.
In love by then
I wanted to survey
The wreckage by myself,
To decide whether loss
Was personal or not.
I couldn't find him
But the sound and the bright
Red fur followed me home.

Since then Spring
Peepers went under the wheels.
The butterflies of Nebraska

Became the dust of my grille.
A bird in Quebec
Dove at my head.
The windshield shattered
Like diamonds
Or cobwebs.
I had the eye
Of a fly
Who views everything
A thousand times
In the gaudy prism
Of possibility
Where we are all food.
And I rode through death
On leather and gas.
In a world of love,
Clean as a whistle,
I float to Paradise
In a slaughter
Of small things.

Aunt Laura Moves toward the Open Grave of Her Father

You are coming toward us
As if you have done this
Every day of your life.

You are stumbling. You are my
Aunt, our ignorant, old fool
And you are completely in

Black. We are, to put it plain,
Putting grandfather into
A hole in the ground. We are

dry eyed as dry ice is cold.
We have made it clear to you
How much you did wrong, how much

Better we could have done al-
Most anything. Except this.
This perfection. This grief.

You are in black. You are moving
Toward us. You are wisdom,
The dark that stabs me at midnight

On any street because I
Am who I am and we are violent
At the horrible, hard gates of

Paradise. You are an army
Of crepe, onyx. Like the wind
You move curtains of sorrow,

Simplicity, toward us.
And I love you while Grandpa
Slips now from our fingers for

Ever and I take your hand
And we hold on together.

IV

The Witches Hammer

I

Only you could do it,
Bring me here,
Or so I imagine.

You move your hand
And the trees fall back
In a full circle.
I lie down in the center.

You smile.
I want to throw you
My skin like a blanket—
Touch me
And I am a mushroom
Erupting through asphalt,

That powerful!
And I wish you would keep me
But I am falling
Into the ground
Like dirt.

II

And all the dear dead things
Laid down,
Writhing on the hook
The bitter fish
Takes whole,
Break water,
Suffocate.

Baited with dirty
Death,
Take up the hook
Dear neighbor,

Out of this dirt of
Bones
Broken, the tree grows.

III

Look, I have met you again.

And look,
You have gone away.

You have done that
Nicely

My disappearing, magic trick,
My ritual.

I hunger for applause and I
Get it,

I march
Like a king down those clapping

Corridors
Because, my God, you are

Yourself.

Good Friday

I knocked on wood.
Good luck's a door,

I thought. What's shut
Will open up.

Wood was the floor
Where once I stood

To look about—
The bridge drawn up

In space drawn down
To let me pass.

Wood built my homes
And covered me.

Cut from the tree,
The iron of grass,

Luck's kindness comes
Out one by one.

High on that place
We hanged with nails,

We choked with blood,
Perishing flesh.

We hammered good
To good. Like a wish

That ends a tale
By coming true,

Struck through and through,
Grace held up grace.

Easter: Boston

Yesterday you were not here,
Nor were you thought of,
Nor did it matter.

Now I have met you.
The chairs and the tables
Rearrange themselves round you
To give you more room.

The old romantic
Horizon widens a bit
And gives you a space
To walk through.

Today I am a little less
For not having imagined you
Who are always yourself
With or without me.

Tomorrow I give out cards
In the subway to your friends,
The total strangers.
I draw arrows in the street,
Chalk lines to your front door.

This is the best I can do
For your love
And your kindness,
To bend with good humor
If only one day,
To the fiction of loving,

To all that it meant
To have met you—
I, who am learning
To welcome you all,
To widen the days.

Making the Parable Bearable

We start by reciting over
The familiar but terrible story.
The king in control of the castle
Without reason poisoned the queen.
The prince ran off with the groom
Of his younger, much-loved sister.
She went weeping to her room.
For one hundred years she sang
And sang his name and no one came.
Father (who cared) was now in jail.
His wizard under the strain went numb,
Entered a monastery, corrupted everyone.
In the end, a moron delivering a parcel
To the court, acclaimed as savior,
Was begged to take the kingdom.
And he took it. Remember,
We're promised no blessings,
No profitable, watchful keeping.
The social fabric became undone.
Absolutely no one won.

Let's run the story once again
To see if we can get it right.
The king dispatched the queen
For some betrayal we must not tell.
A stoic would have gone unhinged.
The prince knew something we do not:
Princess and her beau could not be happy.
Besides, her singing out of grief,
Written down, would make her famous.
The wizard in the vacant abbey
Sifted out the false vocations.
The idiot the court made king
Refused to carry grudges. His reign,
Marked mainly by his long vacations,
Gave all the kingdom vast relief.
Now we have some reasons why,
A little balance in a list of pain.

The countryside submerged in gloom,
The upside-down, abruptly broken lives,
Ringed by motive, now seen fair.
A light goes on inside the tale.
We let the moralists prevail.

Still there's one more way to balance it
And, in between, the pieces fit.
The queen explained her case in private
To the king, and though unhappy,
They shared the power and grew up.
The wonderful stag party finished,
The prince and the bridegroom returned.
That summer the princess and her love
Picnicked under a topiary tree,
Laughed, and almost mended things
And loved each other in their way.
The wizard took his life in hand,
Left prophecy and magic spells,
Built a hut and lived on honest work.
The moron, not stupid altogether,
Founded a delivery cartel.
Optimistic compromise won out,
A getting and a giving room.
Something domestic as regard
Took root. As most of us will do,
They learn. They make it through.

My Father Entering Heaven

Has left behind
The women who ruined him,
Has left behind
The women who loved him,
Without a goodbye
He has gone from the men
He called up from sleep
When I lay beside him
Barely a baby tucked into his bed.
My father is entering heaven.

May he have booze, broads,
And pretty boys.
May he lie down drunk
And erect and arise
Without hangovers,
Love whom he pleases
In a place everlasting,
Without complications.

Whatever he was
Let him be so,
Only grown perfect.
He is a boxer
Brave and unbloodied,
A lumberjack
In a heaven
Peopled by trees
Dying to fall.
Let him cook
As he did at his end
For angelic relations
Eating and drinking,
Applauding forever.

My father entering heaven
Behold me here
In the world

Halfway to heaven
Drunk with the love
And the hate and the fear
Of the heaven
You leave me
If I can take it,
If I can catch you
Flying before me
Faster than light
Into the space
Where you leave me,
Waving before me
A greeting, a glory
Receding. Your booze,
Broads, boys, lumberjacks,
Boxers and cooks
May heaven grant me
Passing to heaven.

Oh, my father entering heaven,
Be there to catch me.

SAINTS

A Little Song for Sainte Mary of Egypt

She was Cairo's golden whore,
An endless and revolving door.
    You know the kind.
    They'll steal you blind
If passion weren't a one-night stand,
The kind who'll lend a helping hand
    And only charge a modest fee.
    For nothing good is ever free.
Sainte Mary of Egypt, pray for me.

Well, she thought she'd take a little trip.
She'd cruised so much, she thought a ship
    Would give her rest.
    She was thrice blessed.
The Captain, First and Second Mate
And all the crew became her freight.
    She sailed to holy,
    Happy ground by sea.
Sainte Mary of Egypt, pray for me.

When they cheered her off the boat,
She started her holiday all afloat,
    Two inches off the ground,
    Her name renowned.
A thousand hearts would not forget.
But in the Holy Land hard-edged regret
    Pushed her back invisibly:
    That special cup of tea.
Sainte Mary of Egypt, pray for me.

All of a sudden, she thought of love,
The thing she knew, God knows, most of,
    The last poor trick
    Where hearts will stick—
And the ground moved up to kiss her feet,
Her prostituted loves went sweet.
    She spun by one degree,
    Shook off idolatry.

Sainte Mary of Egypt, pray for me.

Mary understood how she could skate
Clear cross where most folk love or hate.
    She let her hair grow long,
    Became a hermit for a song.
Dressed in her hair like a little bird,
She perched without a word
    Upon God's tree.
    They let her be.
Sainte Mary of Egypt, pray for me.

I sing you her song because of this:
As there are many ways to kiss
    Or ways to hit
    Or take the bit
Between our teeth, some of us will say
Her first life, or her last's the better way.
    What's that to you or me?
    In spirit or in body
    She loved most liberally.
Sainte Mary of Egypt, pray for me.

Saint Aelred's Dance

They raised him up to serve his king.
    They taught him wit.
    They made him fit
  To serve in everything,
  To conquer with a glance
  The fickleness of chance.
    In song, in dance,
    In *gai musique*,
  He learned to step, to kick,
  To turn, to bow, to trick
His courtly partners into grace.
    His handsome face
    Illuminated space.
      Love, in a word,
      Became his god.
Aelred danced before his Lord.

Good servant that he always was,
    He gave his all.
    He had a call
  To give great matters pause.
  And he loved men.
  It follows, then,
    He drew to bed
    The prince and bred
  With him, instead
  Of kin, the art of love
And all the wonders of
    The flesh made word.
    A love-struck god,
Aelred danced before his lord.

And danced, and danced, and giddily advanced.
    His loving grew
    And not a few
  Entered his heart, and were entranced.
    And loved him more.
    And Aelred saw,

Not that love will go away,
      Merely that it will not stay
And grows and grows each royal day
         And pilgriming abroad
         May hunt out God.
That lovers dance before the Lord.

Thus Aelred hungered for the grace
         That never stayed
         At rest, and prayed
   To spin forever in a dancing place.
         It's not from sin
         He entered in
An abbey on an English hill
And taught us tenderly how will
Will bind with love, but to fulfill
         His self. And God
         Took him as he
         Was and had to be,
         Most happily,
Into his courtly, regal peace,
To please the saints and without cease
   Intoxicate the narrow way.
         Divinely gay,
         His dance, his pay
         For room and board,
Saint Aelred dances for the Lord.

Therese, Therese

How gauche to be so middle class,
 To love stuffed chairs
 And cuddly bears,
To never touch the unwashed mass,
To hug papa, beg his caress,
To play for him the sweet princess,
In short, a bloody, bourgeois mess
Who did what cute young ladies did
 When they were bid:
The absolutely expected.
 To take to bed
When naughty things were said.
 Or feel faint.
 To be a saint.

You drove your family all but mad
 You languished so.
 Made such a show
Of being good you came out bad.
You whined and whined week after week
For sweets that only you would seek
And, adding insult to your cheek,
As if you really couldn't cope,
Went off to tell a busy Pope
To notarize your silly hope
 To be a nun
When you were much too much too young.
And naturally you won.
 What could he do
 With the likes of you?

He sent you to a nunnery
 Your sister ran.
 The thoughtful man
Locked up, thank God, the likes of you from me.
And there you safely carried on and sighed
For Jesus like a doll and played His bride,
His princess and His queen and finally died…

And if you hadn't writ a book,
A fevered, hasty-written second look
At what you comfortably took
    To be some "little way,"
I'd be rid of you, by God, today.
    That's what I'd do
    With the likes of you.

But while bacilli burned your lungs
    And as you died
    You tried and tried
To climb to God by easy rungs.
The only way you'd get things done,
You wrote, was unheroically, one by one:
Let the great leave tiny things undone.
And then you polished up the brass,
Sewed, made beds. And it came to pass
Your little acts gave love great class.
    And though I loved you not a bit
    Who never questioned roles, you sit
    I bet in heaven with a smile and knit
For God six socks that just may fit.
    A little faint,
    To be a saint.

Wilgefortis Now Before Us

Wilgefortis,
Christian princess,

She was beauty,
Daughter, duty.

Her Dad, the King,
Said drop this thing,

Religious,
Inauspicious,

(He was pagan)
This contagion,

Awful folly,
Silly story,

And vow to wed
A pagan lad,

A princely catch
Where crowns attach.

But she would not
And prayed a lot

To turn her grace
Into disgrace,

Her face a haunt
No man would want.

The prince recoiled,
The match went spoiled.

For so God did.
Her face He hid

Beneath a furred
And scratchy beard

And overnight
Set things right,

To overturn
And even spurn

An absolute
That won't compute,

That we make up
And will not drop,

The false sublime
In human time

We not once saw:
Natural law.

Saint Erminold

Saint Erminold was quite the beast,
And drove his monks, and never ceased
His endless, maddening commands—
Until in two stout holy hands
A monk took timber to his head
And, stiff as planking, struck him dead.
The people, who were more perverse,
Prayed to him, of course, and (curse
The ways of Providence) he heard
The tears he would not hear on earth,
Eased many a woman through hard birth,
Guarded the streets the grieving roam,
Would lead the homesick safely home;
In flood brought sun, in drought dropped rain,
Miraculously proved again
While curing cattle, crops, and blight
How desperation may put right.

Saint Augustine

Saint Augustine led a complex life.
Although he had no legal valid wife,
He had a mistress, an invalid son.
She he left behind. The other one,

Adeodatus (or God's blessed gift)
He kept beside him. That pushy family rift
With mother, and her nagging, endless call
To be a Christian (that domestic squall)

Became spring breezes when he took her side.
But then both son and then the mother died.
And Augustine sailed off to Africa
To polish up his saintly character,

Became the Bishop with the honeyed tongue.
Where others preached Augustine sung,
His voice a swan's where sparrows chirped,
His voice an eloquence where others burped.

He died, they claim, his face against a wall,
Full of penitential guilt, while all the while,
Who was that woman that he cast away
After 12 years, two months, one week, a day?

He had a lovely mistress, What's-Her-Name,
Who never reached his solemn august fame.
No love for her, no candles, praise, or fuss
Although I bless her Saint Anonymous.

Dominic Inquisitor

Saint Dominic, as Judge, would take a match
And burn a disbeliever up with straw
Ablaze beneath his feet, or bend and stretch
His limbs apart, or skin her bloody raw

To make the insolent, heretic wretch
Give up the private vision that she saw
And vomit what those personhoods would hatch
While Holy Mother Church made peace by war,

And by these powerful means attach
Good deeds to dreadful ones. How well Dom bore
Into our bones obedience. By such
Tough love he struck us to the fearful core

That keeps us ever vigilant, on watch
For those who break the universal law,
Who will not bend and will not clutch
Dead, dread rules they're running from. Take Care.

Saint Satan

Although he could but poorly name it then,
What dragged him forward was a lust to share.
His backward lonely history mapped smoke and din.
That's when he climbed the hill.
Breathlessly he threw his bulk
Across its top. And shook
Amazed and stared.
He dropped. For once he wept. A haze
Of amethyst swept on
For miles, for miles
The valley ribboned in the sun
A wave of green, a lawn of peace.
That's when he eyed the tree,
The ruby fruit.
And then the two.
He knew he'd never be alone again.
Up on four feet he prowled
To meet them. It was she
He found first. She, he pleaded with.
He knew it was not guile
That made him stammer out,
"Please. Eat. Please. Take."
So then she took,
Brought back the man.
He smiled. The two of them, they smiled. Then stopped.
When man and woman left the place,
He could not think it through
Although he tried.
It was himself who threw
Him down upon his belly. Grief,
Heartbreak made him snake
Behind them ever after,
To crawl to find them
Coupled in a source of loss
Where they felt love

And he heard only oddly
At the end
The sound of laughter.

Angels

What did we do
With them
Once we had caught them?

We wrestled them
Down to the ground
And the mud.
They slipped through our fingers.

Caged,
They flamed into light,
Into glitter.
They danced through the bars.

While we classified
Their obvious difference,
They turned translucent.
They flowed from bathroom
Mirrors,
Shone from our bedroom
Vanities.

Now you are like us, we sighed,
Though they trumpeted difference.

How many are you?
We cried.
Their answer was only a sound
Like wings
Trapped in their feet.

We could not count them
Or find them
Unless they chose
By themselves
To be visible.

Our final escape

Was total denial.
Not from the natural
World, we harrumphed.

While triumph
And secret,
They fluttered
Down to be born
In the family
Transparent
About us.

The Greatest Saint

The Greatest Saint I cannot name.
The few we know of, one and all,
How secretly they sucked up fame.
But Invisible, who heard the Call,

Would, God knows how, have found a path
To make by stealth the Good News new
And do Good Works like higher math
Where none but One could prove them true.

The Juke Box
(uncollected poems)

The Juke Box

The man who lives
in the juke box
juggles his past.

At night he replays
the songs he's collected
in differing order.

Each night,
a new opera.
Over and over,
he swims in surprise.
Over and over,
the stuff
that suffocates him
sings a fresh story.

The combinations,
at last, drive him to tears.
Nothing new here.
Whatever changes
but the order of things?
And he knows it.

He knows the heart looks.
He knows the heart locks.
He presses a button.
'Is that all there is?'
rolls out the juke box.

Under the voice of a song
he well knows
and a singer,
slowly he swings out a note,
pulls out a phrase
of his own.

He lays sound like carpets,

like bedding, like pillows,
adding a polish
that softens the bare ground
he sleeps on
and varnishes stone.

These songs I picked,
he seems to be crooning.
These songs are mine now.

All that's unchanging
he changes by joining.
All that he'll change
changes only by tone,
high note or low.

Silver blue lyrics,
note by note climbing,
tenor and torch song,
he chases the pain.

Just before sleeping,
louder, insistent,
his voice fills the room

with the stretch of his lyrics,
the reach of his range.

Out of the juke box
of songs he's collected
comes the clutch
of the music,
which makes up
to add up to all
that is static
and cannot be broke up,
the calculate
frozen sum of his name.

Saint Mark's Square

He is in the wrong
Place when I see
Him and I cannot
Recall what it is his
Name is nor can I
Move since I have half
Way picked up my
Caffè espresso black
Naturally though he must
Own an entire personal
History come from New
Jersey Manhattan Texas
Even proudly possesses
A wife children lovers
Who knows a history
Who stands like this
Elemental American
Icon under the bronze
Four horses of Saint
Mark imperial salt
Water commerce glass
Or now these Italian
Children pointing up
At him six feet tall
As they do utterly without
Manners at the gold
Mosaic and glass saints
Or anything marvelous
Black burnished alive
Not to throw stones but
To pick out to say 'Look'
There he goes who steps
Out of the square and the
Lives we have bought for
Ourselves or are given
Oh, what was his name?
I would have run up
Or waved or called out

As he went but he's
Gone now and I finish
Lifting the cup to my
Lips the thick coffee
Where my full white face
Like a black mask floats
Free on the surface only
A moment before bright
Bitter revival I need
I remember you American
Black brother Hello
Where was it you went
While I watched and I
Stayed and I rose up
Stood up and spoke
Not one word not at
All this loss after
All and I drink it.

The Axer

His arm, a great
Lover, moves.
The ax falls.
The wood's hard.
Heart cracks and
Cracks, cries out
In a screech
Of splinters.
I can hear
The engine
Of his youth.
He can break
Anything. Whole
Forests fall.
The world moans,
Trees topple.
In my woods,
He labors,
Sweaty and
Mindless of
But one thing:
The harvesting.
The air pounds
With the drum
Of his blows
And the old,
Proud figures
Groan and go
Down. The sky
Blisters and
An army
Of bent men
Plant seedlings
Behind him.
They plant not
To honor giants
Nor repair
Their fluid grief

But merely
To steady
The future,
Or to try.
In heaven
The starry
Machine turns
On the blade
Of indifference
While over
And over
The ax falls
And splits the
Heart of things.

And We Shall Come Rejoicing

They will come, rejoicing,
My students, riding their bikes
Like the girls they maybe found
The first time who like everything
They did, who dress themselves up
In leather and then plaster the
Peace sign all over the place,
Who love speed, get high on poems,
Ride past the stalled traffic
On the highway because they
Are here, who can think but do not
Think too much, for they are rejoicing.

As, in my run-down garden, rejoice
The bees, who do not, either, think
Too much, we think, who drink sunlight
And dust and something from the
Chalice of the herb thyme I
Grew because thyme brews, beyond
America, memories; because the
Greeks grew at the worn-down steps
Of their temples, herbs, chalices, pollen;
Because we may grow drunk on it
All when the bees drink up. Under
Our feet drink, and are rejoicing.

And we shall come rejoicing
Because I drink once a month
With my neighbor and get
Drunk, and remember a little bit
What I am when I'm sober, and
Forget what we said, while my
Poets ride their bikes over the
Road, and the bees go dizzy at
Noontime, and going to work
I am singing, and even then, when
I come home way past dark, when
Only one house around these parts

Has peace written all over it, then,
Neighbor, still, still in the night,
We shall come rejoicing.

The Uses of Mirrors

Although I know
I'm one, singular,

I pursue you still.
Sitting in a bar

I'm twice as far
From myself. Anyone I eye

Smiles from the wrong
Side of their face.

I spy reversals,
The royal flush,

A blush, the other
Side of the deck,

The turned near cheek.
I enter a new room

Endlessly bending
In the glass to pass

My selves, left
Handed, left ended.

In my friend's eyes
I see twin me's

Go blue in the blue sky
Of his iris, and float

Inside out, two sties,
Or stars to travel by.

Still I rotate
In the small round

World of all he
Reflects. Like the dead

In photographs,
I may stand or sit,

Be strong or desperate.
No matter what,

The negative comes true.
Somehow there's two.

In bathroom mirrors,
My hands reverse.

I brush my teeth,
The strongest

Part of my bones.
The visible shines.

The rest stays hid.
I shave backwards

Every morning to cut
Close to the skin.

I drink clear tea
To catch the clever

Reflection of an other
Rise up like hope,

Or like a hangman's rope
(two sweet possibilities)

Inside a plastic cup.
I hang a mirror

Up above my bed,
That well-mapped crossroad

Where I cancel
Singleness awhile,

Where I've reflected
Two more easily

Though single file
And simply done.

I've cherished one.
I've come, deflected,

Doubled, dizzy,
Home, repeatedly

Been seen and seen
And not once caught

The fracture clean:
What is and what is not,

The mirror's common
Place and common scene.

Numerology

*The world is governed by the
power of numbers.*
—Pythagoras

Once upon a time
If you think

About this
In the dark,

You were more.
What's a coupling?

Even to do it
There must be two.

Three's a musical
Movement,

A small band,
The grand

Gesture of
God multiplied.

Four and five
Are a litter

Of puppies,
Several nations

Acting in concert,
A family

Worrying about
Its future.

Six stands

Alone,

A perfect number
And the buzz

Of creation.
Tomorrow's

The breathtaking
Silence of

Sabbaths,
The wonder of

Resting, the
Holiness

Of seven.
Over our graves

Stonecutters
Chisel eight

Personal
Parenthetical

Digits.
From then to now

There's no end
To our counting,

Only two
Staggering

Powers ∞
And the other

We shape

In ∞'s

Presence.
Surprised on the

Sill of love
Or standing in

The amazing
Lobby of some

Old terror,
We pucker up

Our lips
Like children

Mouthing the
Circular O.

He

My tongue upon this man
Tastes salt. In surprise

And thirst together
I drink the water of his eyes.

Taste, who worships where she can,
Takes the local weather

Of his body and the ride
Upon him like a sailing boat

That glides or bucks but needs
The sea he is to keep afloat

Upon a brand-new tide.
Like everything that seeds,

A fountaining, a rise,
A willing more to lift, than,

Failing, fall. And there he lies,
His body open to what breeds

Upon him. Mindless of threat
Or promise, he thrusts on out

In wave on wave the sail inside
And beaches on the world without.

The Photograph

Then
I sit
On the porch
Of morning.

Love
Comes down
From the bedroom

To take my
Photograph.

Across the water
The sun
Through the lens of
One grey cloud

Clicks in a rush
Of sunlight.

The hills
Ripple in a green
Wave

And the lake
Grows roots
Like a blue tree

In a stone
World.

Now
I sit
On the porch
Of the photograph

Taken by love.
Behind me
The paint

Of the farmhouse wall
Peels
And the window,

Bent into
Laughter
And breakfast,

In the sheen
Of pure
Reflection

Glazes.
Here
The sky

Descending
The hall
Of the valley

Surfaces

And the light
Lighting at the lip
Of the glass

In the focus
Of love

Before me

Shines.

The Male Madonna

Rock hard cock
Of the block
Self made man
Made master
Of the jack
Hammer ham
Fisted tough
Piston legged
Lover of
Your son hold
Him tight light
Light of your
Heart's Chamber
On your bent
Arm brick wall
Macho mean
Eyed drop down
Beat drum beat
Feet home sweet
Shepherd's crook
Kind father.

Prayer for a Young Man

Let's face it squarely and without disgrace.
The young man hunts his father in the face
Of men he wrestles playful down to bed.
He courts, embraces, but he does not keep.
It is his father loves him in his sleep
And haunts to claim incestuous a place
Among the lovers where he's left alone.
In bars, in leather and in boots,
In costume and in chase, a change
Comes on. He grows. He preens. He puts down roots.
It's in disguises he will now be known,
And if he's lucky, and if luck come down,
Will find among the masters whom he'd tame
And imitate one singularity who'll break
And crack in voice alone, who'll call his name.
Then may his father's ghost limp costumed home.
Then may love hold him up for once. And take.

Bagging Autumn Leaves

Some things that come with autumn do not change.
Once you've felt fall once, you smell the chill,
not feel it. Half-remembered cold seems strange.
But green goes gold. Or red. And leavings spill

a paper rustle cross the driveway and the lawn.
As ever, we rake leaves the same, and feel
the weight each gathers as we pull upon
the pile we lumber when we haul the real.

Years past, my father and I made a mound.
We took a match and turned the leaves to flame.
A smoke and incense fumed the neighborhood around.
Like sacrifice, we immolated every year the same.

I smell those years, burnt spice. My father's dead.
I did not wrap him greenly up when I let go,
but like the leaves the trees obscenely shed,
I carried him in smoke and ash to snow.

Alma

Dressed in red, my aunt looks through her sliding door.
Outside the balcony, the world glares green,
Floridian. The sun blares down a howl of yellow ore.
She looks unmoved upon the seething ferment of the scene.
The rot and riot which means growth will come unseen.
If she's not here to see it, what matter that growth goes
Or comes? The present is the presence that she knows.

In granite Maine, a gray, less complex shore,
She married, conceived her children. Into that mean,
Cold evergreen, she bore necessities she hungered for.
The winter Atlantic kept her conscience lean.
The snow, the ice, made any cutting edge of love more keen,
More clear. Then cancer came. Inside that flow,
Her cells divide: the pain her watch keeps turning to.

Meanwhile Northeast turns August to the core.
Up North the summer's lust does not admit decline,
Diminishment, or to smooth flesh gone wounded raw.
What means a place where she's no longer fleshly seen?
High in the tree, the leaf first touched by frost can screen
Away all summers: one alarmist blood-red leaf can glow
The glory of the fall to come, the grip and rip of undertow.

191

Students as Autumn Leaves

Or a Sonnet of Double
Resignation
Built on a Cliche

Leaves sift like snowflakes from the tree,
Shift underfoot, but keep from reach.
So in your classrooms you could see
The sometime students whom you teach,
Or whom you try to, drop from view.
They listened or they listened not,
And showed that, indeed, they knew
Or diligently would not be taught.
We know. We know. The teacher's grace.
But if the ghosts of students passed,
Or flunked, parade your dreams, or race
Like tie-died leaves tied down at last,
Recall some number will remember
That who they are means where they were.

For Vic and Skiff
November 30, 1988

The Mandarin's Recitation

What we are to learn are
Details: the sun rises at 6:34,
Sets at 4:23, High Tide, 8:35 a.m.,
Low, 2:31 a.m. There's only one
Of the one but two of the others.
Be sure you know this. The heart's
But a beating muscle, enthusiasm
A vapor I cannot construct again.
When the transport is over what you
Need is a ticket, diploma, degree
In engineering. The concrete can be
Absolutely manipulated, like shame or
Guilt or failure. Only the almanac
Has a tight memory. Like the heart.
No need the half moon rising on
Your thumbnail. No need 29 ½ days
Menstruation and the tide pulling
And pushing between zero and this
Place. No need at all. The stocks
Rise and fall: 8/52, 2/31, 29/5,
Numbers are all, the language of
Much of it, of God the pundits say,
The $E=MC^2$, too, and what of that when
Language or goodness or love terminally
Has nothing to do but deconstruct
What mother and father anciently
Said quite clearly was: No
Thing at all. Now. Let's be
Quite clear. Clinical. What's done
Is done. I give you the vein.
Construct. Put blood in it.

The Nuclear Virgin

For Ginger

The Virgin Mary in a blood-red robe,
Stained by the pomegranate of the Lamb's
Cut throat, lets loose a glance sharp as a probe
Sparked from within the nuclear I AM WHO AM.
Like arcs on vacant lots or penal yards,
Like ovens glowing in exterminating camps,
Her eyes shine spotlights shadowless and hard,
Her incandescence an atomic lamp.
We formulate within a sapphire whirl
Of mossy green, beneath the pure snow white
Of ice blue cold. Our evolutionary curl
Of Earth crawls upward into cosmic night
While on her solar and celestial arm
Ignites her new born Son's abyssal calm.

Infant Jesus

By kneeling down, we get to see close up.
An oil lamp hisses, spits and spills gold light.
You nest inside it like a golden drop,
A bead of butter in a blacked-out night.
Incense of milk, warm caramel and blood
Slips from your lips and slips, each breath, small sighs,
Small wrists and fists. Around you, dung, hay, wood,
Cold stone. A cough. You open up your eyes,
And look unfocused all around, wide-eyed.
We look into that look and catch a glint
Where we're reflected where we watch outside.
You close your eyes. You sleep. "What has it meant?"
"That's but the lamp we saw." "That was His star,"
We say, that fired fleck, that turn of nebula.

Saint Joseph Genitor

You ground in legend as a young old man
Whose Galilean nights were trouble-tossed.
You walked away before your boy began
To really work. Not standing at the Cross,
You're leaning elsewhere but not there. Up and gone,
Straight-forward Daddy once removed, lost boss,
He'd love you all the more, your Dad-less son
Who'd spin to twist Our Father out of loss.
Saint Joseph lean. Earth is your walking stick,
Where double helixes revolve and spin
Where ruby DNA, a glowing wick,
Will flower lilies out, the virgin in.
Green grows your brown and wooden niche:
Your foster fathering of stars coils in.

Decade

Which is to say Garden Bloom a rosary
Is around and a round wreathing a Virgin
Virgo, Virago of the Wedding Feast Lady
Oh, lately miraculous changes grapes to wine
Grey Clay bandy-legged cups Gold Chalices
But vinegar too Loss tossed in the flower of
Hope THAT glitter crown corona chrysalis
Madrigal minuet mazurka Love
Waltzes everywhere in in tears spectacularly
Profligate useless cocoons hummingbird
Loon cassowary divine ninnies multiply
Would you not say so the beautiful words?

Winter Solstice

Level as a lead bowl
by day, we call day light.
By night,
one lone radiance of owl.

Too Hoo. To who?
To whom belongs
this snowy moan?
This claw and cull and calling moon?

Who catch this thing?
Icy caul, fall, tin ping,
thin gong,
wound up metallic spring.

Sex

For Larry M.

Blood tells.

The silken
Uncoiling serpent
Finally bites.

Fangs in the wrist,
Needles in the bone.
They will not cut out.

The looking glass
Where he found himself
Shatters.
Now he walks barefoot
On cut glass.

Everywhere
The same cry:
Protection.

After the lavish
Summer,
The headstones
Line up

Like white flowers
In a harvest
Of stone snow.

Old Man, Old Heart

Old Heart,
Why in our cozy faithlessness
Did we turn into this alley?
Why are we not tramping
Down familiar streets
To force our neighborly
Seductions on these we
Slept with from pity?
When we two turned adultery
Into a kind, if cold, place
Where the defeated could
Defeat only each other,
Why are we out here
Swelling with obsession?
Why did we turn
From the kind faces
That suffered with us?
Why are we fondling
The thighs of young girls,
And breathing hard over
The bodies of young men?
What are we trying to rock
Into life
Or to sleep,
Old Heart?

Old Man,
We have just learned
We are dying.
Missing our youth
We pretend to be with them.
They are not wisdom
But we will feed on them
For a time like gluttons.
They will break our hearts
And be blameless.
Thus we suffer their coy,
Gay beauty like a penance

For all we once wronged
In the wonder of our own
Childhood where others
Smilingly perished.
And, too, when they consent
To love us, they'll carry us
Like a tattered flag
At the head of an army
Into all their battles.
Let others look astonished
At how worn out we are.
We are beyond pain
When we love them.
Against all that most
Surely is coming,
For these small moments
We two will linger
Over what their kisses
Slipped onto our tongues,
Beyond thrill or love,
Anaesthesia,
Old Man.

The Watchman

He learned again
Like a child how
To climb down the stairs
After his stroke,
How to sit on the front
Steps of a street
Full of pastel houses.

In his pocket he kept
Three peanuts to feed
The pigeon who roosted
Over the eaves. Always.
One at a time.

He saw the street
Up and down as a place
Where people belonged
Or didn't. Overweight,
Winded, he sat in
The shade of a tree.

When the city cut off
The lower branches
Of the tree that kept
His shade, caught in the hot
Sun, he leaned on his cane
Climbed up the stairs
To the chair in the living
Room and stayed there.

The pigeon circled
The steps waiting for
The peanut he would give.
One at a time. Always.

"I am living on borrowed
Time," he told his son
At Thanksgiving. His wife

Who had once hoped of
Being a nurse, bathed
His swollen legs. One
At a time. By being
Trained for service,
She later recalled,
She had realized her dreams.

In December he heaved
Himself up from the chair
To greet the visiting nurse
Who was pleased with his progress
And care. But he fell.
His heart broke and he
Did not even cry out
But cracked and died at once.

The neighbors looked for him
Out of habit. Then went on
Their own way. One at a time.

Out of habit for a time,
The pigeon circled the front stoop.
For months, one man
On the way to work
Watched the bird continue
To circle and circle
And circle. One at a
Time. One at a time.
And then disappear.

The Grand Hotel

The room always appears
adequate though slightly novel.
You examine the prints on the wall
picked by some anonymous master hand.
You throw open the drapes
or the sliding doors to admire the view.
There are clouds in the sky,
couples arranged in the atrium.
It will have to do. You unpack.

Later you notice there are rules,
regulations. "You are here,"
says the sign. You inspect the corridor
for the exits, just in case.
"No Smoking." You head for the bar,
buy a drink, steal an ashtray.
Afterward in your room,
awash in a suddenly secret vice,
you smoke up a storm.

In time this is the place you live in.
Nothing is strange. Everything fits.
By now, however, the meetings are over,
the conferences finished. Time to go.
You glance about to see what you've missed.
You leave with what you came with,
plus some complimentary cologne
smelling like incense, postcards,
some plastic magnetic memories
to glue to the refrigerator.

In the lobby the concierge,
the housemaids, the bellboys
line up with their hands out.
You tip them. "Nice stay," you assure them.
The limousine spaciously rolls up,
long as a hearse but barren of flowers.
On the road to the terminal

you take one long last look
as the landscape rolls by.

On the plane you recline and wait.
"Fasten your seatbelt," smiles the attendant,
sweetly solicitous. "Have a nice flight."
You hear a roar, feel a lurch like acceleration,
a lift and a rush. As you close your eyes,
you imagine you rock on the wings
of a bird that hurtles you like a stone
or an arrow into the night,
back home where you come from
and where you belong.

Reading Lips

Once I used to live in town.
I wandered all the streets around
scavenging for things unfound
(ecstatic raptured walkabout).
I'd wall all in
in cul-de-sac.
All want. All need.
That was me,
dead end alley and free.

I'd sort yards out.
I'd find refuse trash to keep,
something surfaced from the deep.

I collected dross like wealth,
bartered cast-a-ways by stealth.
I found me talking to myself.
I promenaded puffed indeed.
In every eye I found an us.
Each eye looked back
anonymous.

Now I live away from there.
I work and play at solitaire.
A bird gone sleepy in his cage,
I walk a cold late autumn beach
and feel my heart
still skip a beat
but now from age
and not from love
nor from summer's heat.

I jog my solitary sport
and run about to be alone, apart.

Now I talk to me myself by choice.
And should you bend to overhear
(come near, come close)

wherein my monotone,
unnamed, unclaimed,
you'll find therein
some you I babble of.

The Man on the Next Roof

The man sits at the edge
Of the roof reading. We must not
Come up behind him and suddenly
Pat him on the back. Nor must we
Yell in his ear, Fire. Startle.
Who knows what might panic
Out of the open book in his hand.
Maybe the book itself will trigger
In his mind some sorrow capped
So deep he will stagger upward
Sobbing, forgetting how easy
To rise only to fall to the ground.
Perhaps some old fear or failure
Will come perfectly realized
Into his mind, some remembered
Ecstasy of God, a first love,
And he will walk onto the air
As if it were water and plummet,
This man, solid as stone, who sits
At the edge reading a book.

Orpheus Sings

You cannot hear me
in the daily din,
among the horns and clatter,
cars, buses,
subway trains,
the chatter.
Urgent matter
packs you in.

But when you lie
at 3 a.m.,
tormented out of sleep
or craving light,
I am the rising dawn
you cannot see,
the dreams you drift upon.
I am the music coming on.
I am he.

My fingers
that flow down
through your hair,
my sigh that brushes
past your ear,
you misconstrue
as breeze.

On moonless nights,
my lush blue green
awash the shore,
just out of sight,
you hear as sound
and think the sea's.

Behind the glow
in morning fog,
almost found
but always,

always
out of reach,
find me.

These concrete notes
that fill the page
you can collect
and recollect.

But when I play,
my strummings
that won't stay
relay
those single lines
into a place
like classic grace
where we
entwine,
align
into design
and as I will I spill
(into the common clamor,
the incessant stammer)
my untimely glamour.
Harmony.

One moment
that you can't recall,
when you were looking
elsewhere,
there not here,
deeply buried and engulfed
in someone else,
in self,
I eyed you all alone.

I stole your name,
your solitary tone.

I carry you along.

Outside of time,
besieged by rhyme,
I let you live.
I give.
You will not die.
Dust and ashes
fall away,
yesterday, tomorrow, and today.

I make you song.

ABOUT THE EDITORS

KEVIN GALLAGHER is a poet, publisher, and political economist living in Boston, Massachusetts with his wife, Kelly, kids Theo and Estelle, and dog Rexroth. His recent books of poetry are *Radio Plays*, *And Yet it Moves*, and *Loom*. Gallagher edits *spoKe*, a Boston-area journal of poetry and poetics. He works as a professor of global development policy at Boston University.

MARTHA COLLINS is the author of nine books of poetry, most recently *Night Unto Night* and *Admit One: An American Scrapbook*. She founded the Creative Writing Program at U.Mass-Boston and served as Pauline Delaney Professor of Creative Writing at Oberlin College for ten years. Her tenth book, *Because What Else Could I Do*, is forthcoming from the University of Pittsburgh in fall 2019.

CPSIA information can be obtained
at www.ICGtesting.com
Printed in the USA
BVHW031949090419
545086BV00001B/2/P